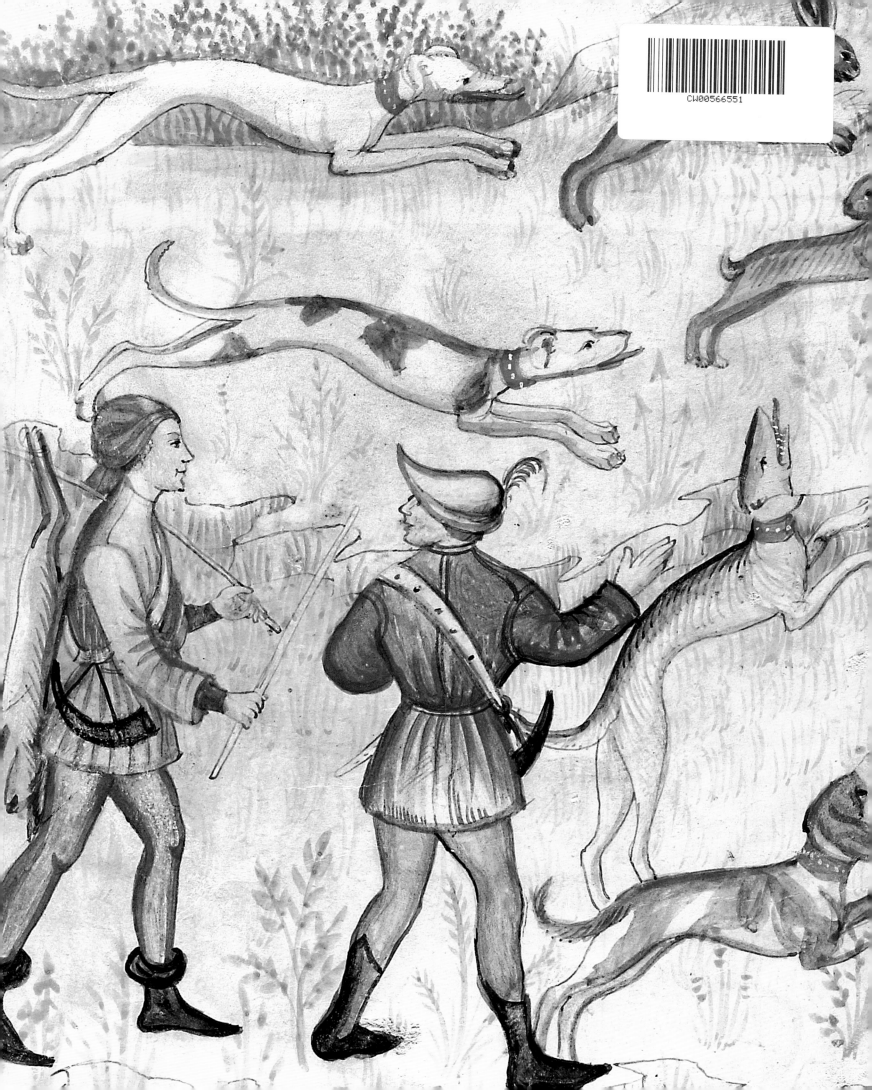

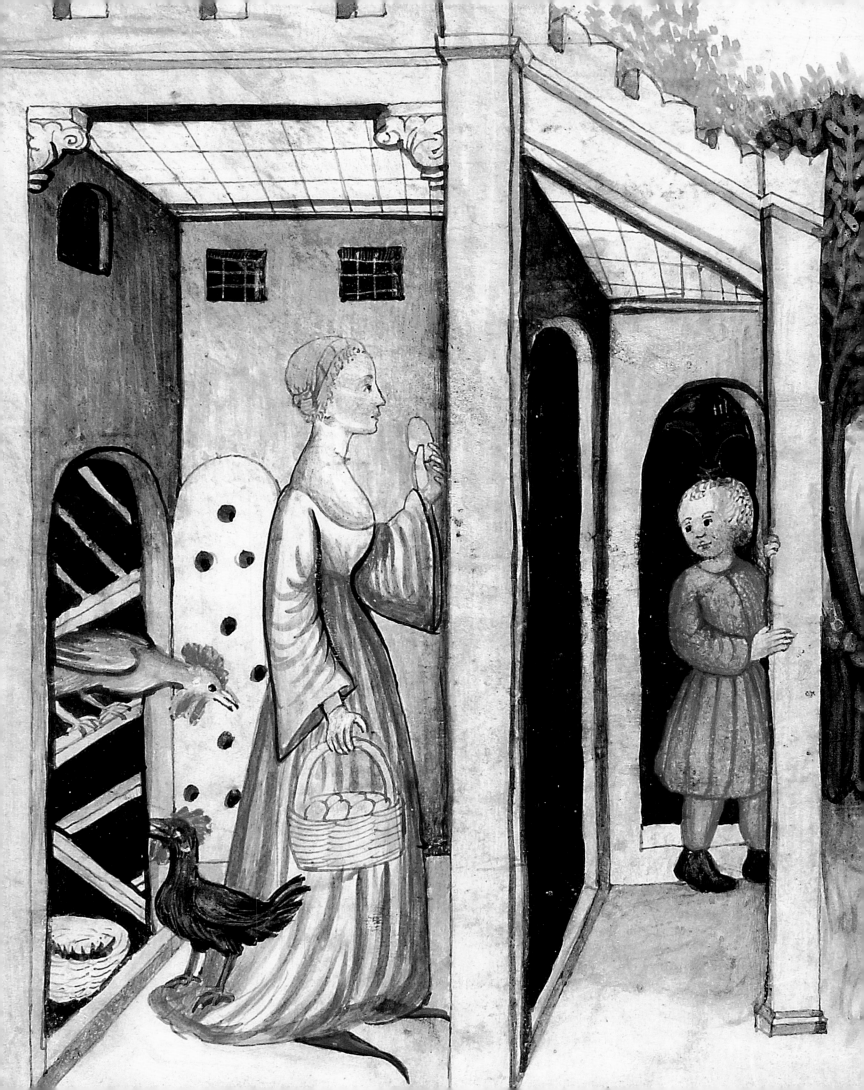

Tacuinum Sanitatis *An Early Renaissance Guide to Health*

ALIXE BOVEY

SAM FOGG
15d Clifford Street
London W1S 4JZ

TEL. 020 7534 2100
FAX 020 7534 2122
EMAIL info@samfogg.com
WEBSITE www.samfogg.com

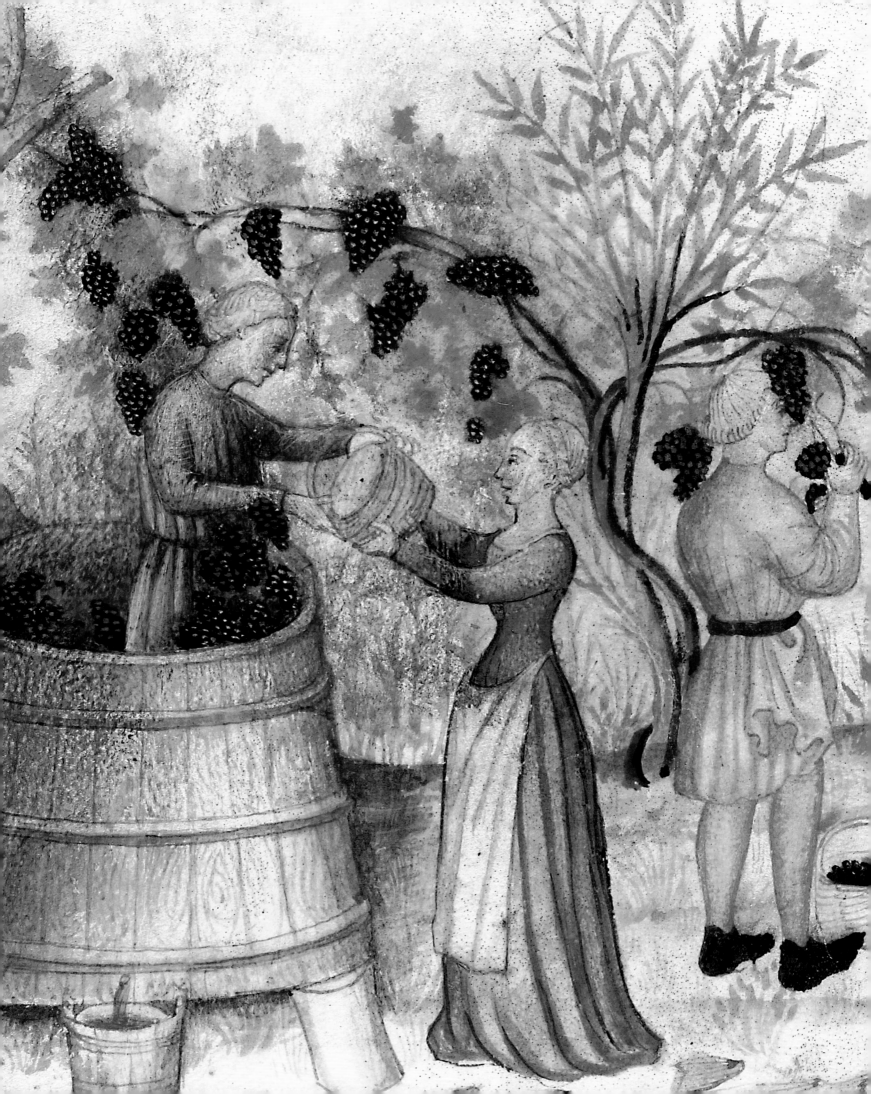

This book accompanies
an exhibition of miniatures
from the Liechtenstein
Tacuinum Sanitatis
at Sam Fogg
15d Clifford Street, London
1–29 July 2005

Contents

A Note on Conventions
Unless noted otherwise, all illustrations are of the
Liechtenstein *Tacuinum Sanitatis*. References to images from
the Liechtenstein *Tacuinum* relate to their catalogue number.

Feniculuſ

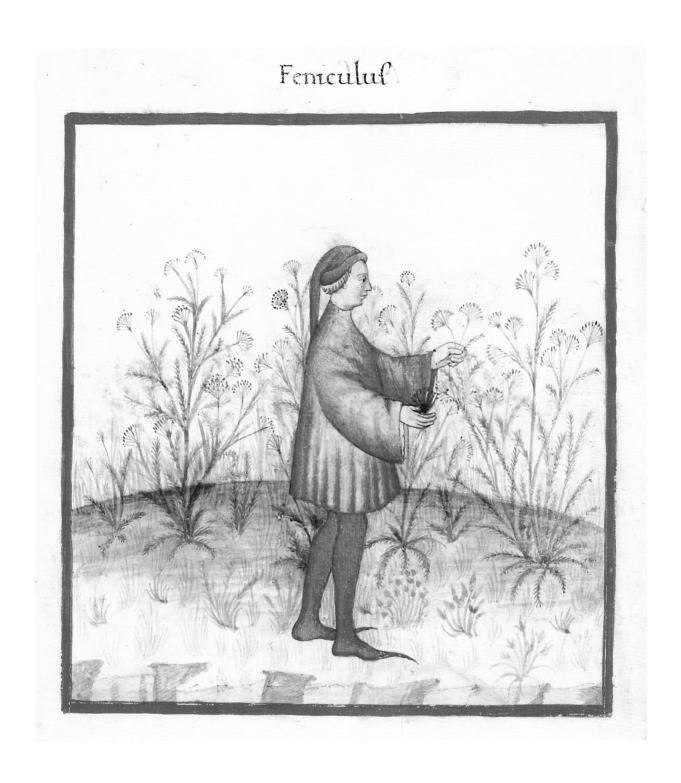

PLATE 1 Fennel

An elegantly dressed man picks a sprig of fennel, which is good for the eyesight and an effective remedy for fever. The iconography of this image closely follows that of earlier *Tacuina* (compare, for example, fig. 7), but subtly updates the gentleman's dress by raising the hem of his tunic to above the knee and giving him long pointed shoes. *No. 14*

Fructuſ mandragore

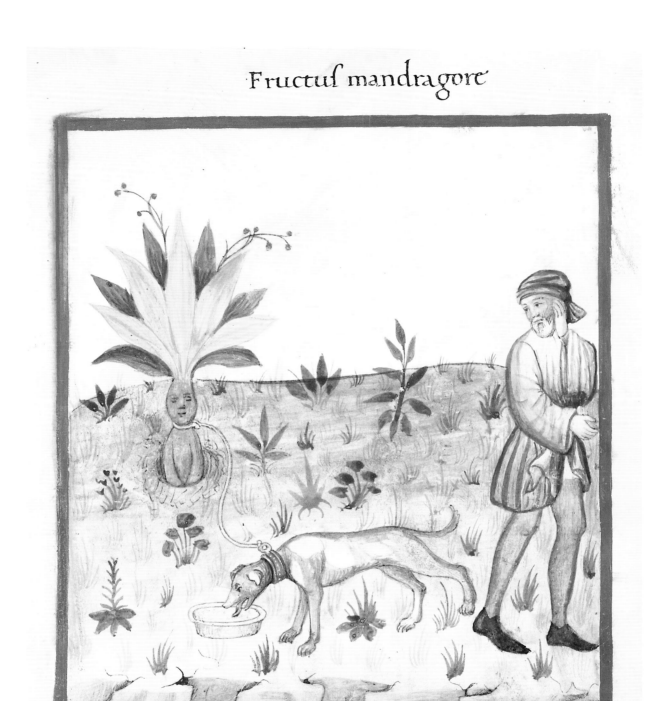

PLATE 2 **Mandrake**

According to ancient lore, when a mandrake is uprooted it lets out a chilling scream. In this miniature, a man has tied his dog to the mandrake so that the dog can pull the plant out of the ground, thus saving his owner's hearing. The man hurries away and covers one ear to protect himself. The iconography of this scene relates to a pictorial tradition established in Late Antique Herbals. *No. 10*

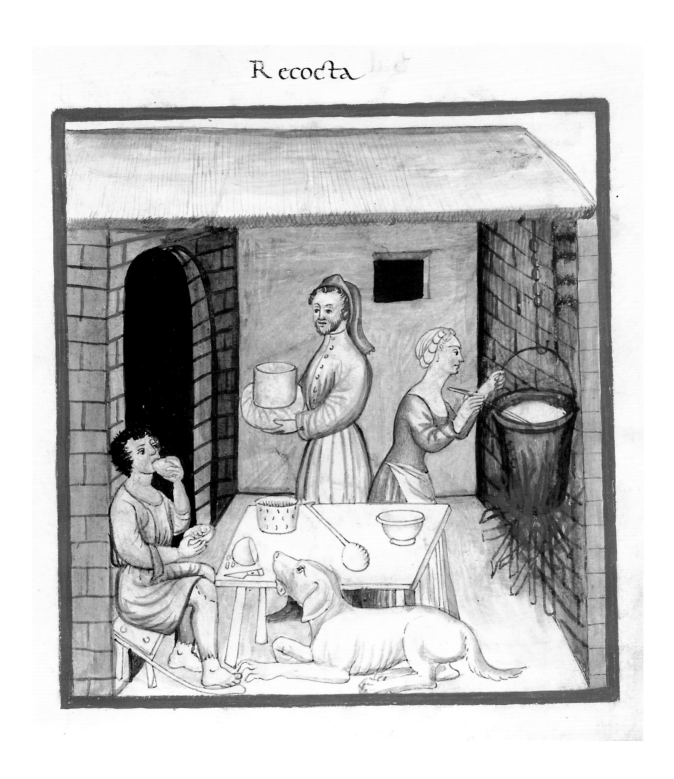

Recocta

PLATE 3 **Ricotta**

This is one of several scenes in the Liechtenstein *Tacuinum* to be set in a domestic kitchen. Here, a woman makes a fresh pot of ricotta cheese, stirring it over a fire, while a man offers food a beggar who sits on a low stool. *No. 54*

Tri

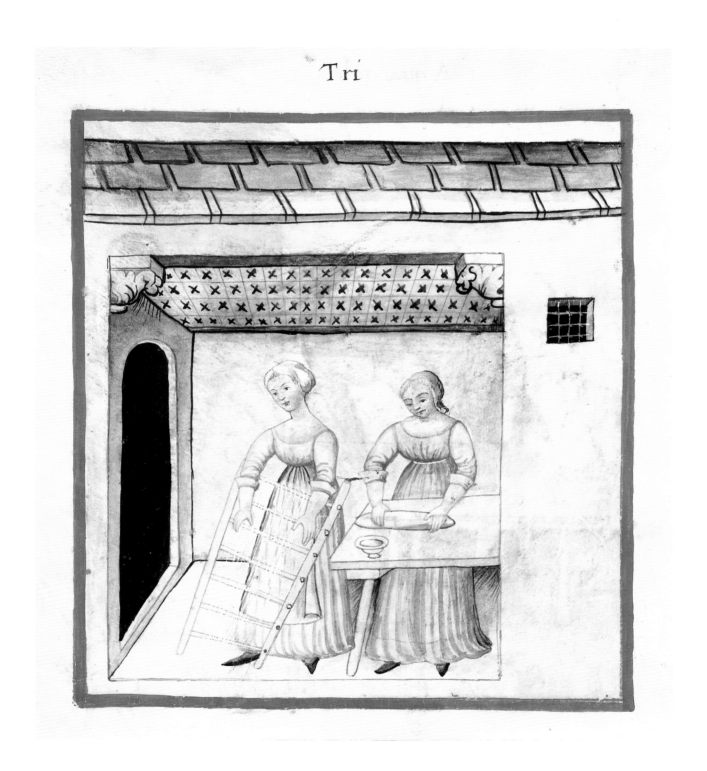

PLATE 4 Pasta

The title for this miniature is *Tri*, a Latinization of the Arabic word for pasta. This reflects the ultimate source for the *Tacuinum* in the Arabic *Taqwīm* of Ibn Buṭlān. In the miniature, two women make spaghetti, one rolling out the dough and the other placing the noodles on a drying rack. *No. 38*

Milium

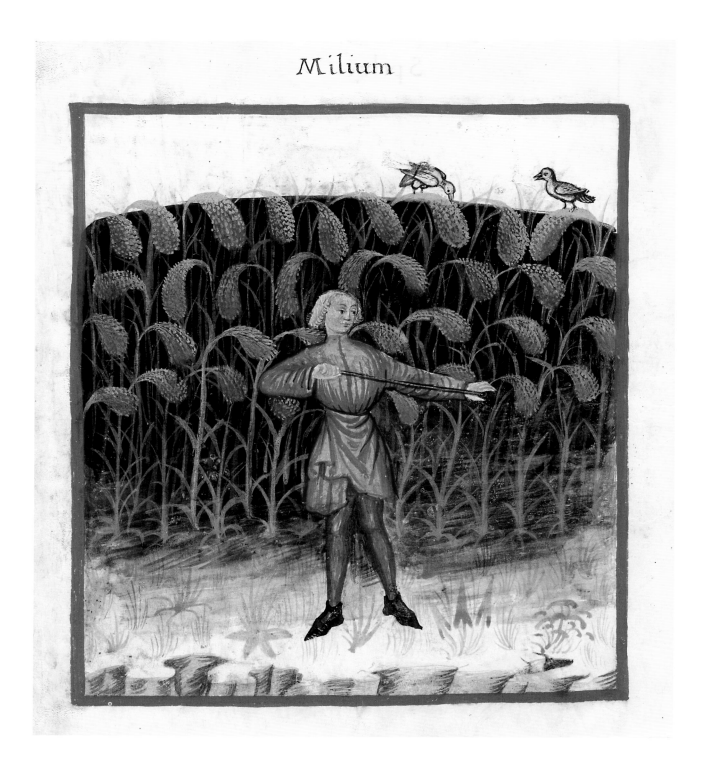

PLATE 5 Millet

Birds feed on millet seed, impervious to the finely dressed man in the foreground, who gestures with a cane, presumably trying to stop the birds from devouring the crop. *No. 40*

Panicum

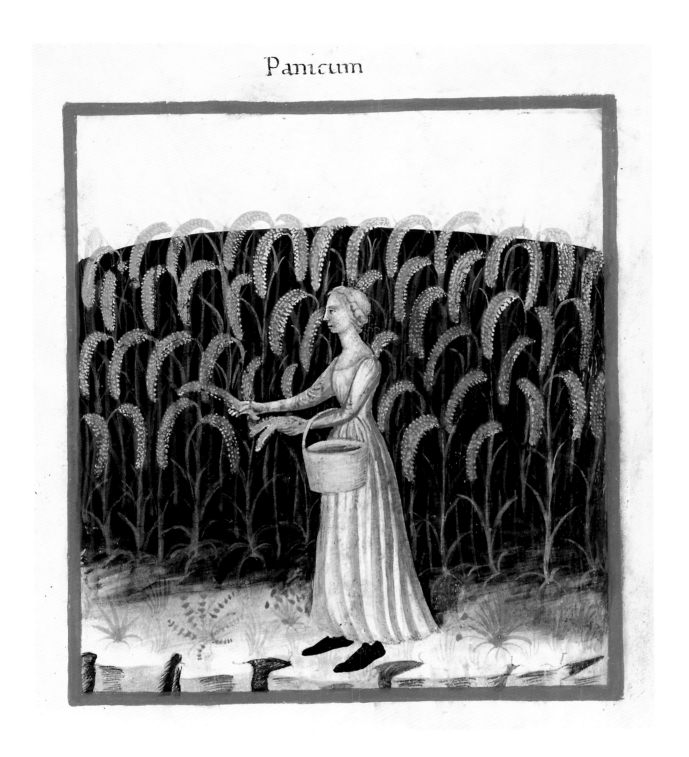

PLATE 6 Panic grass

A woman gathers panic grass (also known as Italian millet) in a basket. The best panic grass has large ripe grains. *No. 41*

Cargagelarum & capriolox

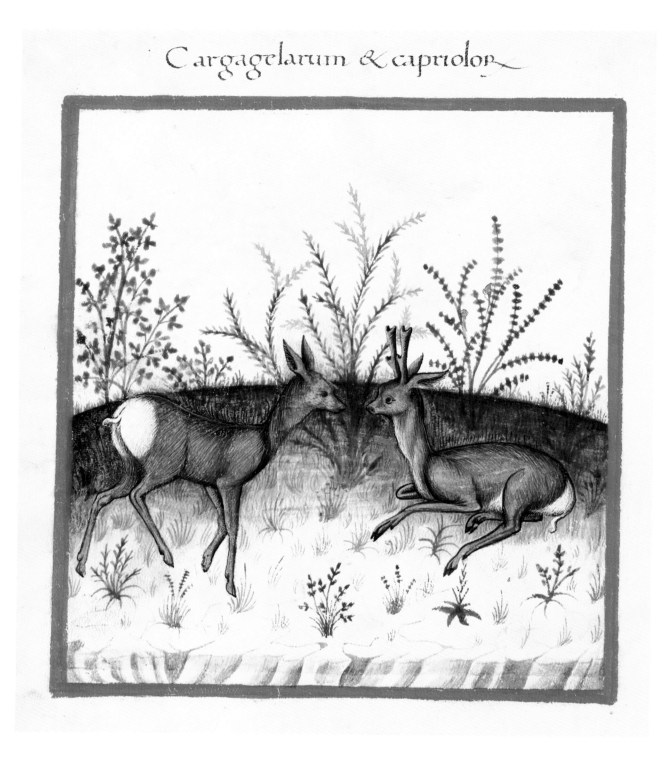

PLATE 7 Deer

A doe trots towards a stag that sits in a verdant landscape. *No. 63*

12

Anatef & anseres

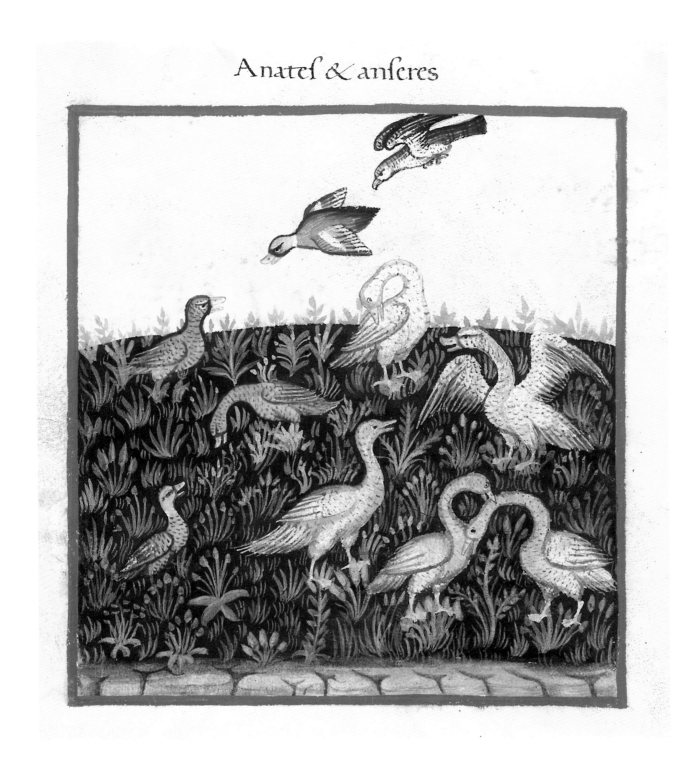

PLATE 8 **Ducks and geese**

A hawk chases a duck, which flaps down to take refuge in a field of ducks and geese. It is recommended that melancholics should eat such birds in order to fatten themselves up. *No. 60*

TAcuinu sanitatis de sex rebz q suit neccie cuilibz hoi ad
cotidiana psuationem, sanitatis sue cu suis ratificatoibz & opatoibz.

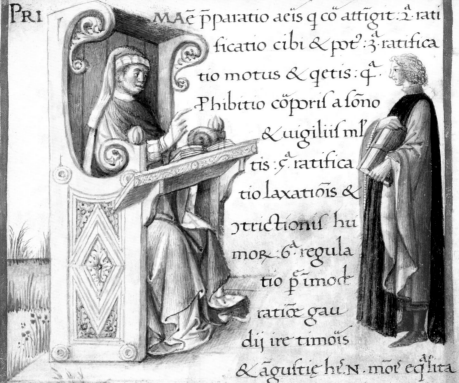

PRI MAE pparatio aeis q co attigit. 2ª rati
ficatio cibi & pot. 3ª ratifica
tio motus & qetis. qª
Phibitio coporis a sono
& uigiliis mlã
tis. qª ratifica
tio laxatiois &
ptrictionis hu
mor. 6ª regula
tio pimoti
ratice gau
dij ire timois
& agustie hi. N. moi eqªlita
tes erut psuatio sanitatis & remotio istorum sex abhac eqlitate
fca egitudiez, do pmittete gloioso & altissio & sub qlibz horum
genere se plures spes & plui, neccie qre dicem natuã. Si dco pla
cueit. Dicem & lectioes puenietes cuilibz sm pplexionem
& etate ipi & oia ponem ilibo eo q mlti loqa sapietum
aliqñ fastidiut auditozes & diusitates mltorum librorum opposi
tor. Hoies. N. nolut descientis in iuuamta no pbatioes seu
diffinicioes. Ideo itetio nra ihoc libo e abreuiae smoes plixos
& aggare modos diuersorum librorum. Attme nri pponti e
no recede a consiliis antiquorum medicorum.

Tacuinum Sanitatis
An Early Renaissance Guide to Health

The Secrets of Health

The Tacuinum Sanitatis *concerns the six things which are necessary for every man for the daily preservation of his health, with its regulation and its operation.*

These are the opening words of the preface to a remarkable copy of a guide to health for lay people. This richly illustrated manuscript was made in North Italy, probably in the city of Padua, in the 1450s [fig. 1]. In the nineteenth century, this manuscript was divided into two parts, one now in Rouen's municipal library and the other in London.[1] These parts belong to a small group of lavishly illustrated manuscripts made in northern Italy between the late fourteenth and the mid-fifteenth centuries of the work known as the *Tacuinum Sanitatis* (literally, 'Table of Health'). The *Tacuinum Sanitatis* provides guidance on all the things necessary for a healthy, happy life, including advice on eating, drinking, sleep, entertainment, clothing and climate.

Translated from an eleventh-century compendium by the renowned Arab physician Ibn Buṭlān, the word *Tacuinum* is a Latinization of the Arabic word *taqwīm* (meaning 'table' or 'almanac').[2] In the Arabic *Taqwīm al-sihha*, Ibn Buṭlān provided a comprehensive overview of the foods, drinks, activities and environments that, according to the traditions of ancient Greek and Roman medicine, would ensure good health. Arranged in a series of forty tables, Ibn Buṭlān's guide immediately became popular in the Arab world. In the thirteenth century it was translated into Latin, thereby re-introducing the West to its own medical heritage, systematized and simplified for the benefit of the literate layman. In the fourteenth century, the tabular *Tacuinum* was reconfigured as a picture book, with copies owned by patrons such as the Visconti family.

Depictions of alarming treatments such as bloodletting, cautery and surgery in illustrated medical treatises are potent reminders that being a patient in the Middle Ages was a high-risk activity, requiring bravery and faith in equal measure. The juxtaposition of images of the Crucifixion with scenes of a physician treating patients suffering from gruesome abdominal injuries in one fourteenth-century treatise seems to suggest that both doctor and patient ought to pray for success [fig. 2]. The *Tacuinum* approaches health from an entirely different avenue: its aim, set out in its preface, was to provide

Fig. 1 Preface to the Liechtenstein-Rouen *Tacuinum*, showing a physician lecturing a well-dressed gentleman on the six things necessary for good health. *Rouen, Bib. Mun., MS 3054, f. 1r (B)*

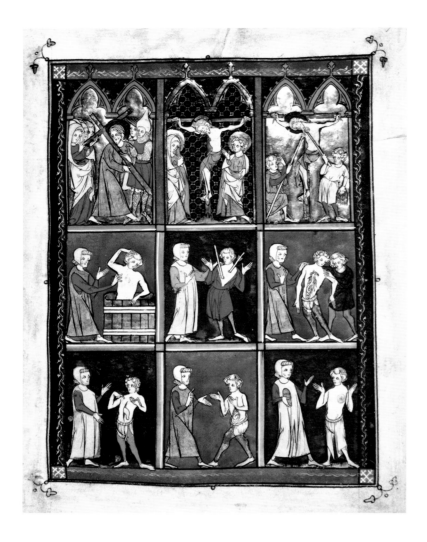

Fig. 2 Three scenes from the Passion of Christ juxtaposed to six images of a physician tending patients with various injuries. From a copy of Roger of Frigardi's *Cirurgia*, France, *c.* 1300–10. *British Library, Sloane MS 1977, f. 7r*

laymen with information that would help them to maintain good health and cure minor ailments through diet, exercise, environment and the regulation of emotions. Its focus is on prevention rather than cure, and its claims for effectiveness appeal to scientific knowledge (however spurious) rather than divine intervention. A large part of its attraction to readers may have lain in its unspoken promise to help them avoid unnecessary encounters with the professional physician.

The Liechtenstein *Tacuinum*, named for the family who owned it from the late nineteenth century to 1948, is the only illustrated copy that remains in private hands. It represents subjects ranging from farming and butchery to sex and sleep disorders. But it is much more than just a record of early Renaissance health advice: it is also a rich seam of pictorial information about everyday life, depicting activities such as shopping, collecting eggs, conversation and making spaghetti.

This study traces the roots of the Liechtenstein *Tacuinum* in Antique and Arab medicine, explores its relationships to the other illustrated *Tacuina*, and also examines its content and its post-Renaissance history. Additionally, all of its miniatures are reproduced and described, accompanied by a new edition and annotated translation of the Rouen *Tacuinum*'s preface by Crofton Black, a list of the manuscripts attributed to its scribe by the late A.C. de la Mare, and a concordance of the miniatures in the Liechtenstein and Rouen volumes.

The 'Six Things' and the Ancient Origins of the Tacuinum Sanitatis

The medical concepts that underpin the *Tacuinum Sanitatis* originated in ancient Greek and Roman medicine, specifically in the body of work associated with two men, the Greek physician Hippocrates (c. 460–377 BC) and the Roman physician Galen (129–200).

Hippocratic and Galenic medicine recognised a kinship between the four elements (air, water, earth and fire) and the four bodily fluids, or humours (blood, phlegm, black bile and yellow bile), and contended that the correct balance of these substances was necessary for health.[3] Each of the four humours was associated with a particular temperament or *complexio*: sanguine (blood), phlegmatic (phlegm), melancholic (black bile) and choleric (yellow bile). The humours also correlated to the four seasons, the four ages of man (infancy, youth, adulthood and old age) and the four qualities (hot, dry, cold and wet) [fig. 3]. An imbalance in the humours could result from a variety of causes, including disease, diet and seasonal variation. Winter, for example, was wet and cold, and stimulated the overproduction of phlegm. Therefore, to correct this imbalance, hot and dry substances were prescribed.

In the turbulent transition between Antiquity and the Middle Ages, most of the Hippocratic and Galenic corpus disappeared from the Latin West, along with much other ancient learning. This knowledge may have been forgotten in the West, but it was not lost: much of it was preserved in the Arab world. From the ninth-century caliphate of Harun al-Rashid (*reg.* 786–809), a campaign to translate works in ancient Greek into Arabic took shape. Within this project, Hunayn ibn Ishāq (died 873), known in the West as Joannitius, was a central figure, locating and translating with his pupils 129 Galenic texts into Arabic. As a result of these efforts, more works of Galen today survive in Arabic than in their original language.[4]

In his introduction to one of Galen's texts, Hunayn ibn Ishāq (Joannitius) explained that medicine was divided into the theoretical and the practical, and that theoretical medicine was further divided into three: that concerning the naturals, the non-naturals, and the contra-naturals.[5]

The naturals included the elements (air, water, earth and fire); qualities (moist, cold, dry and hot); humours (blood, phlegm, black bile and yellow bile); members (including the brain, heart, liver, testicles and so on); energies (natural, spiritual and animal); operations (including appetite, digestion, retention, expulsion, desire); and spirits (natural, vital and animal). The contra-naturals were disease and its causes and consequences. The six non-naturals encompassed climate; food and drink; movement and rest; sleep and wakefulness; elimination and retention; and the emotions. Proper regulation of the six non-naturals, Ibn Ishāq explained, would maintain the health of those prone to illness.[6] According to this theory,

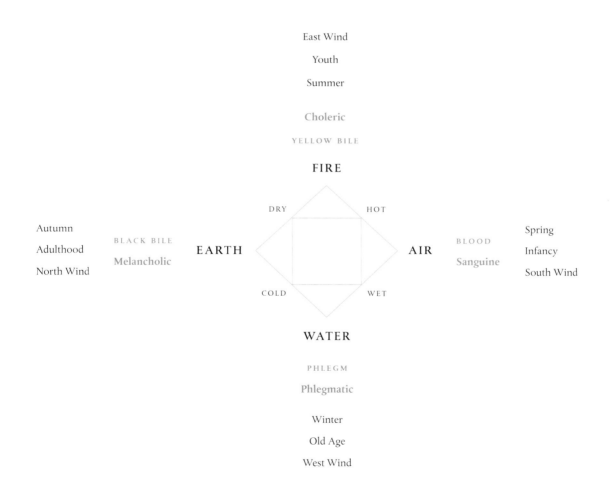

Fig. 3 Diagram of Fours: Elements, Qualities, Humours, Ages, Temperaments, Winds and Seasons

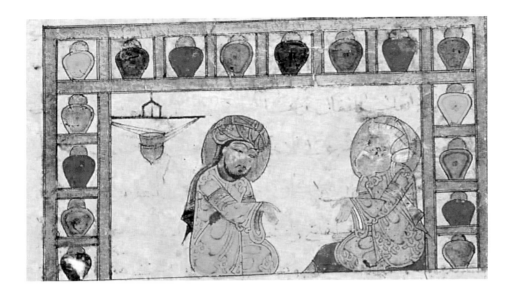

Fig. 4 Two physicians, possibly Ibn Buṭlān and Ibn Ridwān, in dispute, from Ibn Buṭlān's *Banquet of the Physicians*. Probably Syria, dated 1272. Milan, Biblioteca Ambrosiana A. 125 inf, f. 5r

the naturals were the substances that made up the body, and the non-naturals were the external elements that affected its health.

The translation of these ideas into Arabic not only benefited learned medical professionals, but also laymen. Several important treatises based on Galenic thought were aimed at a wide audience, with tracts such as 'He Who Has No Physician to Attend Him' by Razi (died 925) explicitly intended for the ordinary reader.

In this spirit, al-Mukhār ibn Buṭlān (died 1063), a Nestorian Christian physician, collected together all the material he could find on the six Galenic non-naturals [fig. 4].[7] In the preface to the resulting work, Ibn Buṭlān explained that lay readers only want to know the results of scientific enquiry, rather than to read long scientific debates and definitions.[8] Adopting a format hitherto used principally for astrological almanacs, Ibn Buṭlān organized 280 non-naturals into forty tables, laid out across facing pages. The tables summarize the properties and effects of these non-natural substances, with sections devoted to particular categories, such as fruits and their varieties (table II), fresh and salted fish (table XVII), and the changing of the air according to the winds and seasons (table XXIX). Each entry consists of a brief account of the substance's nature; degree; best variety; usefulness; risks and how to neutralize them; advice concerning the patient's temperament and age; regional and seasonal recommendations; a citation of authorities; and a few sentences of general advice.

Ibn Buṭlān's *Taqwīm* proved an enduringly popular manual in the Arab world, and slowly its influence extended to the Latin West. In the thirteenth century, some two hundred years after Ibn Buṭlān's

death, it was translated into Latin. Inscriptions in two fifteenth-century manuscripts contain slightly different accounts of the translation's patronage. One of these manuscripts begins: "Here begins the book of the *Tacuinum*, translated from Arabic into Latin at the court of the illustrious King Manfred, lover of science".[9] Manfred was King of Sicily from 1254 to 1266, and his court was located at Palermo. Another *Tacuinum* contains an inscription stating that the manuscript was translated by 'magister Faragius' for King Charles.[10] This Faragius (also known as Farragut) translated several works for Charles of Anjou, King of Naples and Sicily (died 1285).[11] In either case, the Latin *Tacuinum* seems to have emerged from thirteenth-century Sicily.

With the translation of Ibn Buṭlān's *Taqwim* into Latin, a complex body of Galenic medical knowledge had effectively been systematized, re-packaged, and delivered to the Latin West in a form that could be used by physician and layman alike. Evidently, the Latin *Tacuinum* in Ibn Buṭlān's tabular format was a popular work, surviving in more than twenty-five manuscripts and appearing in print for the first time in 1531.[12] The process of adaptation, translation and dissemination that marks the transformation of the *Tacuinum* from its ancient sources into Arabic and then Latin continued in the fourteenth century, when the *Tacuinum Sanitatis* was adapted as a picture book.

The Pictorial Tacuinum

In the late fourteenth century, the *Tacuinum Sanitatis* was transformed from a rather utilitarian set of synoptic tables into a richly illustrated manual intended for the perusal of wealthy lay men and women. In these pictorial *Tacuina*, an entire page is devoted to each non-natural. Each page is dominated by a miniature illustrating the subject, accompanied by an abridged version of the corresponding text in the tabular *Tacuinum*. A core group consisting of five pictorial *Tacuina* survives, presented here in the order in which they are thought to have been made:

1. Paris, Bibliothèque nationale, MS nouv. acq. lat. 1673[13]
2. Liège, Bibliothèque de l'Université, MS 887[14]
3. Vienna, Österreichische Nationalbibliothek, cod. ser. nova 2644[15]
4. Rome, Biblioteca Casanatense, cod. 4182[16]
5a. Rouen, Bibliothèque municipale, MS 3054 (Leber 1088)[17]
5b. *Olim* Liechtenstein; London, Sam Fogg

These richly illustrated books originated in Lombardy, perhaps through the patronage of the Visconti, the lords of Milan. The copy in Paris, made *c.* 1390–1400, was probably owned – and perhaps commissioned – by Verde Visconti (died *c.* 1405), the daughter of Bernabò Visconti and wife of Leopold III of Hapsburg [fig. 5]. The *Tacuinum* in Liège is attributed to the workshop of the Milanese painter and illuminator Giovannino dei Grassi (died 1398). It is believed to have been executed around the turn of the century (*c.* 1390–1400) for Giangaleazzo Visconti, who usurped control of Milan from his uncle Bernabò in 1385.[18] The *Tacuinum* in Vienna (*c.* 1385–1400) belonged to Georg III von Liechtenstein, Bishop of Trent from 1390 to 1419, and is thought to be one of the manuscripts listed in the 1410 inventory of the goods seized as war booty by Friedrich IV, Count of Tyrol (1386–1439) [fig. 6].[19] The patronage of the *Tacuinum* in the Biblioteca Casanatense in Rome is unknown, but it is closely modelled on the Vienna manuscript and was probably made relatively soon after its exemplar was completed [fig. 7].[20]

Ownership of an illuminated *Tacuinum* would have conferred the distinction of possessing the kind of book that only the wealthiest could afford. Yet the pictorial *Tacuina* are not just status symbols, nor are they merely dumbed-down versions of the tabular *Tacuinum*. The explanatory texts of the pictorial *Tacuinum* are concise, but they contain most of the information present in its tabular source.

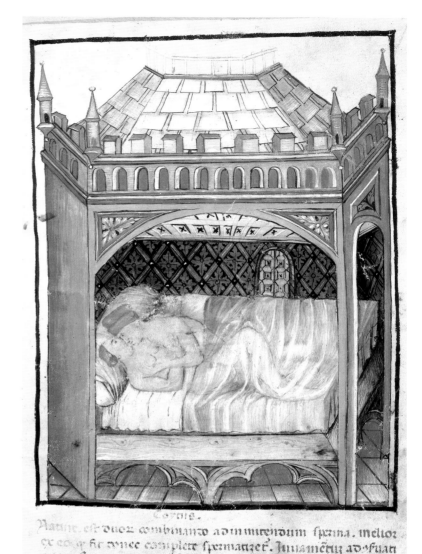

Fig. 5 The illustration for coitus in the Paris *Tacuinum* is much more explicit than that in the Liechtenstein copy (compare no. 124). *Paris, BnF, MS nouv. acq. lat. 1673, f. 100v*

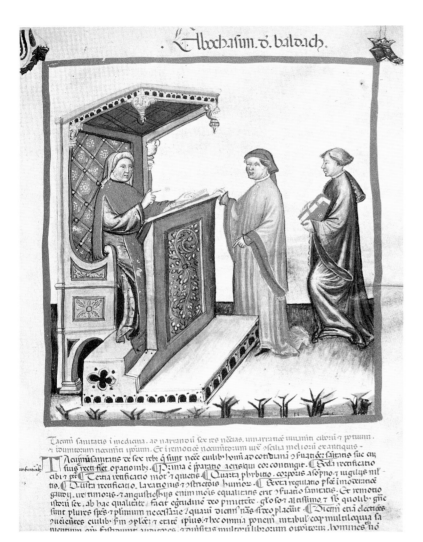

Fig. 6 Preface to the Vienna *Tacuinum*, showing the author, Ibn Buṭlān (identified in the inscription as Elbochasim of Baldach), explaining the purpose of his text to two gentlemen. *Vienna, ÖNB, cod. ser. nova 2644, f. 4r*

Information in the copies in Liège, Paris, Vienna, Rome and Rouen is generally arranged under five headings:

NATURE (*natura*): the dominant quality of the substance in terms of its hotness, wetness, coldness and/or dryness
OPTIMUM FORM (*melior ex eo*): the best variety or part to use
HEALTH-GIVING PROPERTIES (*juvamentum*): its benefits
DANGERS (*nocumentum*): potential harmful side-effects
NEUTRALIZATION OF DANGERS (*remotio nocumenti*): how to counteract side-effects

Additionally, the Vienna *Tacuinum* provides advice about the patient's age and temperament, and the season and region in which the substance is found.

If the aim of the tabular *Tacuinum* was to condense information into a few charts, the pictorial *Tacuina* had a rather different purpose. In these *Tacuina*, each subject was given its own page, complete with a large miniature accompanied by a succinct account of its nature, effects and risks. The resulting manuscripts are grand, lavishly illustrated volumes. Undoubtedly, the most important element of the pictorial *Tacuinum* is the images, which enrich its textual content both aesthetically and practically, helping the reader to tell the difference between, for example, horehound (no. 2) and wormwood (no. 3), or helping to recognize a lupin (no. 22) by its leaves alone, even without its distinctive floral raceme.

Its rich cycle of images, many of them depicting plants, fused the *Tacuinum Sanitatis* to another type of book, the illustrated Herbal.[21] Descending from an Antique tradition, medieval illustrated Herbals contained information and images of plants and, sometimes, minerals and other substances. From the thirteenth century, their popularity grew rapidly. Interestingly, an inscription in an important thirteenth-century Herbal reveals that it was owned by Manfred of Sicily, the probable patron of the *Tacuinum*'s translation into Latin.[22] Although there is some overlap between the material covered by Herbals and the *Tacuinum Sanitatis*, the purpose of these two types of books is distinct. According to Minta Collins, the *Tacuinum Sanitatis* is "in a category apart from the Herbals because the elements included cover a wider field and have less medical applications".[23]

It may be that someone like Verde Visconti or her cousin Giangaleazzo owned a tabular *Tacuinum* and valued its textual content, but found themselves continually needing to consult a Herbal to find out what specific plants looked like. Frustrated by the need constantly to flip back and forth between two books, such an owner could well have come up with the idea to commission an illustrated *Tacuinum*. Charged with this task, artists would almost certainly have consulted illustrated Herbals in order to devise the programme of illustrations to accompany the text of the *Tacuinum*.

A magnificent volume known as the *Historia Plantarum* in the Biblioteca Casanatense in Rome demonstrates cross-fertilization between Herbals and *Tacuina*, and shows that the two types of book could be found in the same libraries.[24] The *Historia Plantarum*, an encyclopedia of plants and related subjects made *c.* 1394–95, was produced in the workshop of Giovannino dei Grassi, also responsible for the Liège *Tacuinum* owned by Giangaleazzo Visconti. Interestingly, there is much evidence to suggest that the *Historia Plantarum* was made for Giangaleazzo.[25] Several images in this manuscript are clearly copied from a *Tacuinum Sanitatis*, complete with their distinctive scarlet borders [fig. 9].

The Liechtenstein Tacuinum

In 1981, it was revealed that the Liechtenstein *Tacuinum* was in fact the long-lost component of the *Tacuinum Sanitatis* in Rouen.[26] When the Liechtenstein-Rouen manuscript was divided, the Liechtenstein volume was cunningly cropped and bound so as to appear complete and distinct (see 'The History of the Liechtenstein *Tacuinum*', p. 30). The pages of the Liechtenstein manuscript are more than 7 centimetres shorter than those of the Rouen *Tacuinum*.[27] The area of their framed miniatures, however, is identical, both measuring about 140 mm x 125 mm, and their page width differs by only half a centimetre (5 mm) or so.

In its nineteenth-century form, the Liechtenstein *Tacuinum Sanitatis* consisted of 68 parchment leaves, including 130 miniatures, two drawings and an index. The Liechtenstein portion was supplied with page numbers in Roman numerals and a forged index of its contents, both in a faux-humanist hand of the nineteenth century. When the manuscript was recently disbound because the deterioration of its nineteenth-century binding was imperilling its miniatures, its fragmentary structure was revealed.[28]

The Rouen *Tacuinum* consists of 56 folios, measuring 243 x 162 mm [figs. 11 and 12]. It includes 70 titles, of which 36 were never illustrated (ff. 35, 36, 37–53v; see figs. 18 and 19). Of its 34 illustrations, one is a drawing (f. 33) and two were, apparently, later additions (ff. 35v and 36v).[29]

The whole Liechtenstein-Rouen *Tacuinum* is the product of a

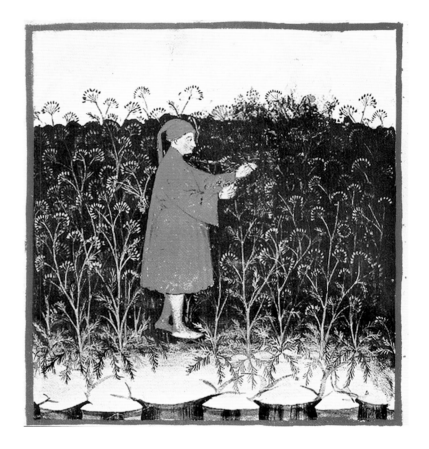

Fig. 7   Fennel, from the Casanatense *Tacuinum. Rome, Bib. Casanatense, cod. 4182, p. LXXVI*

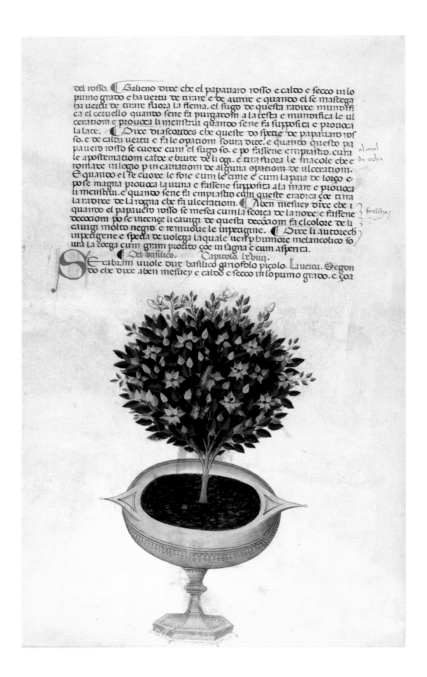

Fig. 8 Basil, from the Carrara Herbal, Padua, *c.* 1400. *London, British Library, Egerton MS 2020, f. 50v*

collaboration between a humanist scribe, discussed separately below, and several artists. Florence Moly Mariotti has shown that the Liechtenstein *Tacuinum* was executed by four illuminators.[30] The division of work among these artists is as follows, listed according to the manuscript's Roman-numeral pagination [fig. 10]:

1) I–IV, VII–VIII, XI–XIV, XVII–XXX, XXXIV–XCVI

2) V–VI, X, XV–XVI, XXXI–XXXII

3) XCVII–CXI[31]

4) CXII–CXXXII

The first artist was responsible for the vast majority of the miniatures (87 of the Liechtenstein *Tacuinum*'s 130 images). This painter's miniatures are painted in washes of transparent colour directly on the parchment. The second artist – the least accomplished in the manuscript – undertook only seven scenes, working in the same technique as the first artist. The work of the third hand is the most distinctive in the manuscript, with graceful, elongated figures with small heads. His accomplished draughtsmanship, relatively ambitious use of perspective and staccato, sketchy brushstrokes set his work apart from that of the others and reveal somewhat more awareness of Renaissance stylistic innovation than that of his collaborators. Unlike the other artists, who painted directly on to the parchment, the fourth artist painted on a thin white ground layer.

Moly Mariotti and others have suggested that the fourth artist may have worked somewhat later in the fifteenth century than the other three, on the grounds that his architecture is more refined and his costumes and interior decoration seem more advanced. It is worth pausing to consider the implications of the suggested interval of a decade or more in the production of the manuscript. All of the Liechtenstein-Rouen *Tacuinum*'s artists relied on an exemplar closely related to the Vienna *Tacuinum*. Like the others, the fourth artist follows compositions established in earlier *Tacuina*. Examples of this dependency on the Vienna-derived exemplar are conspicuous in his miniatures for sexual intercourse (no. 124; compare fig. 5); anger, in which a woman bites on a cloth (no. 115; compare Vienna, ÖNB, cod. ser. nova 2644, f. 98v); and summer rooms, showing a young couple standing on an open porch (no. 113; compare Vienna, ÖNB, cod. ser. nova 2644, f. 97r). Another detail should be taken into account. The fourth artist depicts a distinctive blue fabric patterned with red three times in his series of miniatures (nos. 117, 123, and 130); this fabric also appears in the work of the first artist (no. 85). Thus the fourth artist must have had access not

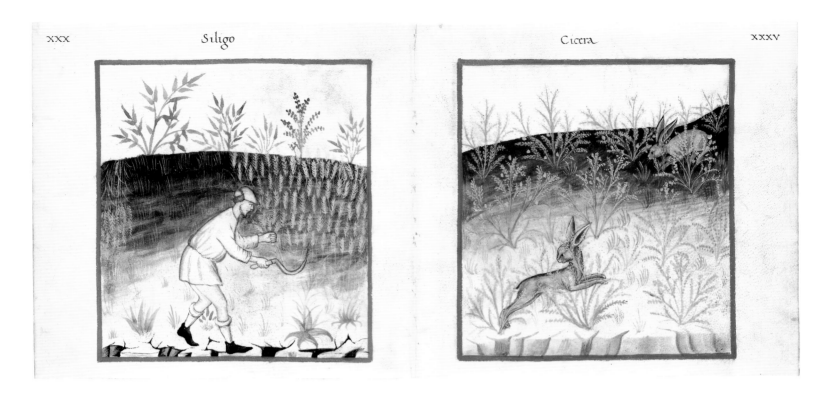

Fig. 9 Bifolium showing a peasant mowing a field of rye and hares frolicking in a field of chickpeas. *Liechtenstein Tacuinum, pp. XXX and XXXV (nos. 44 and 42)*

only to the same exemplar, but also to this same bolt of blue and red cloth. If, as Moly Mariotti suggested, the fourth artist worked many years after the first three painters, then the Liechtenstein-Rouen *Tacuinum* would have had to remain unfinished for many years in the artists' workshop, until such time as an illuminator should again pick up where the others left off. But why would such an expensive, elaborate undertaking as the Liechtenstein-Rouen *Tacuinum* have been abandoned in the workshop and then resumed in this way? It is much more likely that the four artists collaborated in a single campaign, sharing the same exemplar and workshop props (such as the cloth). In that case the differences between the fourth artist and his colleagues would have resulted not from the date of his work, but from his training, his ability and his greater willingness to deviate from his model in details of architecture and dress.

The Liechtenstein-Rouen *Tacuinum* was undoubtedly a hugely ambitious undertaking, conceived to include at least 238 miniatures, 30 more than survive in the next largest *Tacuinum*.[32] Given the intended scale of its cycle of miniatures, it is perhaps not surprising that it was left unfinished. In the Rouen manuscript, 36 spaces intended for miniatures were left blank, with only text and title on those pages. In the Liechtenstein *Tacuinum*, two of the spaces for miniatures were left blank (nos. 7 and 46). At some later date, someone filled in these blanks, rather clumsily tracing the drawings on one side of the parchment on to the other in black ink [figs. 13, 14].

In terms of its style, iconography and content, the Liechtenstein-Rouen *Tacuinum* is closest to the Vienna and Rome copies. Indeed, if it was not based directly on one of these manuscripts, its model must have been. Comparison of subjects such as hare meat and autumn reveal the similarity between the Liechtenstein copy and its ultimate source, the Vienna *Tacuinum* [figs. 15, 17]. Perhaps the most distinctive feature connecting these three manuscripts is a shared propensity to set scenes precariously close to a cliff-edge, whether or not this makes pictorial sense. In the Liechtenstein *Tacuinum*, a barley field is situated on the edge of a crumbling precipice (see no. 35), but so is a rice shop [fig. 16].

The Liechtenstein-Rouen *Tacuinum* includes more than thirty subject headings not found in the earlier pictorial *Tacuina*.[33] Because none of the surviving pictorial *Tacuina* is complete, it is impossible to determine precisely the extent to which the Liechtenstein-Rouen manuscript added to the established programme of subjects. However, given the number of unprecedented titles in Liechtenstein-

Rouen, we can be confident that the Liechtenstein-Rouen *Tacuinum* was not merely a slavish copy of its model, but rather an ambitious project intended to extend and update its scope.

Evidently, many of the subjects in this innovative programme of titles stumped the Liechtenstein-Rouen illuminators. In many cases, presented with the text for subjects not illustrated in their model, the artists were apparently unable to devise appropriate images. The Rouen portion contains 26 unique titles, of which 23 do not have illustrations [figs. 18, 19]. Presumably, unless the manuscript's exemplar came to their aid, the artists were at a loss as to how to illustrate tricky subjects such as *sperma* (sperm)[34] or exotic entries such as *xilo aloes* (aloe wood),[35] the wood of an aromatic tree indigenous to Asia and known botanically as *Aquilaria malaccensis*.[36]

Most of the new titles in the Liechtenstein-Rouen *Tacuinum* are in the Rouen portion, but four are in the Liechtenstein manuscript (nos. 6, 7, 8, and 11). The artists managed to create illustrations for all of these except for marine oregano (no. 7). This page was originally left blank, and was filled in later with a tracing from the opposite side of the page. Sometimes the artists must have found other pictorial sources or drawn on their own knowledge of common plants, such as rosemary (no. 6). One illustration at least shows some invention in the face of an unusual subject. The miniature for sandalwood (no. 8) shows a man fishing twigs out of a stream with a hooked stick and placing them in a shallow vessel on the bank beside him.

A few titles in the Liechtenstein *Tacuinum* use terminology different from that of the other manuscripts. The illustration for junket (no. 53), for example, follows the iconography for the subject *lac coagulatum* (coagulated milk) established in the Vienna manuscript,[37] suggesting that the two terms were considered to be synonymous. It has been suggested that the Liechtenstein *Tacuinum*'s illustrations for *Doctrina* (instruction, no. 129) and *Sponsa* (bride, no. 117) may have been misunderstandings of the titles 'motion' (*Motus*) and 'joy' (*Gaudia*) present in other pictorial *Tacuina*.[38] However, these changes are perhaps better interpreted as deliberate alterations rather than errors: it seems improbable the manuscript's highly skilled scribe, discussed below, would have ignored his exemplar's text and simply guessed at these titles on the basis of their miniatures' iconography. Instead, perhaps the titles 'instruction' and 'bride' were thought to update or otherwise improve the *Tacuinum* for its patron.

Despite the innovations in the Liechtenstein-Rouen *Tacuinum*, it is clear that its artists relied heavily on their exemplar for almost everything, from page layout to style and iconography. While the earlier *Tacuinum* manuscripts were probably made in Lombardy – in centres such as Pavia and Milan – it is more difficult to locate the origins of the Liechtenstein-Rouen manuscript on the basis of its style.[39] The hand in which its texts are written, however, has been identified as that of a skilled humanist scribe, and his career helps us to locate the origins of the Liechtenstein-Rouen *Tacuinum*.

The 'Albi Strabo' Scribe and the Origins of the Liechtenstein-Rouen Tacuinum

Because the style of the Liechtenstein-Rouen *Tacuinum*'s miniatures looks back to earlier *Tacuina* picture-books, it is difficult to place it within the context of the stylistic output of a particular town. However, the hand in which its texts are written offers some evidence of its regional origins. Unlike the earlier *Tacuina*, which are written in Italian round hands, the Liechtenstein-Rouen manuscript is written in a clear, elegant humanist script [fig. 19]. The late palaeographer Albinia de la Mare identified the work of this scribe in a number of other manuscripts.[40] In her description of one of these books, the copy of Leonardo Bruni's *History of Florence* formerly in the collection of Major J.R. Abbey, de la Mare described his hand as "a formal, upright, humanistic bookhand, inclining slightly to the right".[41]

Among the books associated by de la Mare with this scribe is the celebrated copy of Guarino of Verona's translation of Strabo's *Geography* known as the Albi Strabo [fig. 20].[42] In 1459, the Albi Strabo was presented by Jacopo Antonio Marcello, then the Governor of Padua, to René of Anjou. Millard Meiss attributed the manuscript's two miniatures and twenty initials to Andrea Mantegna (1430/1–1506),[43] but this ambitious attribution has not met with universal acceptance. Other scholars have placed its illumination within the sphere of Jacopo Bellini. Lilian Armstrong has tentatively suggested that the miniatures might be the work of Jacopo's son Giovanni (*c.* 1435–1516), and has concluded that the

Fig 10
The four artists of the Liechtenstein *Tacuinum*

Clockwise from top left
Sage, by Artist 1 (p. IV, no. 4);
Vegetables, by Artist 2 (p. XXXII, no. 23);
Yellow wine, by Artist 3 (p. C, no. 101);
Betrothed couple, by Artist 4 (p. CXXVI, no. 117)

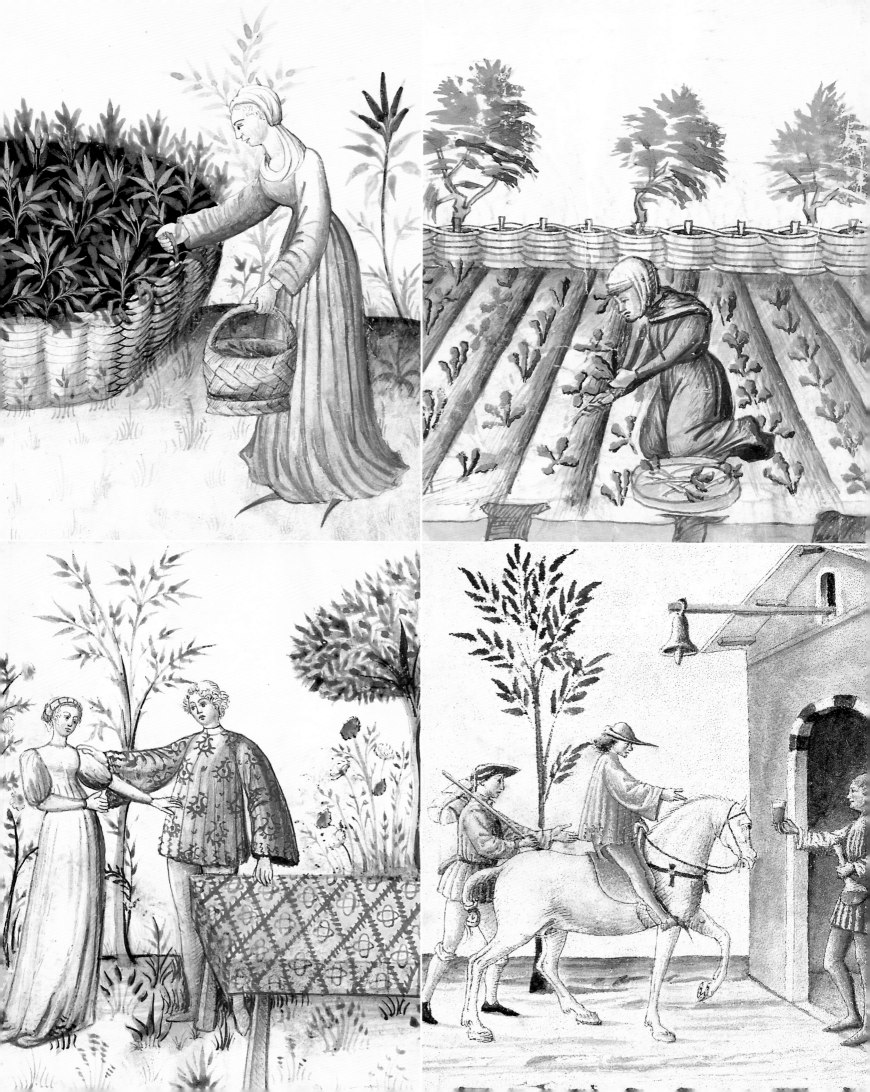

Fichuf

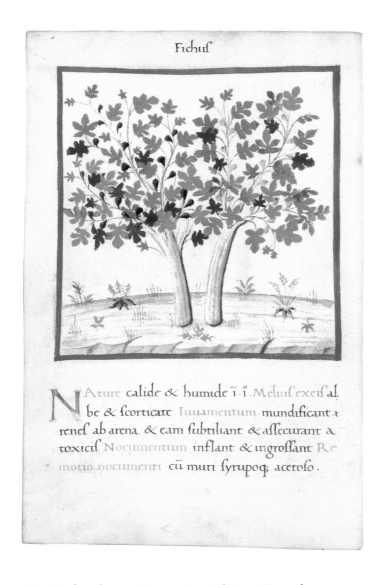

NAture calide & humide ī i̇ Meluf exeif al
be & fcorticate Iuuamentum mundificant ẋ
renef ab arena & eam fubtiliant & affecurant a
toxicif Nocumentum inflant & ingroffant Re
motio nocumenti cū muri fyrupoq̃ acetofo.

Portulaca & citareia

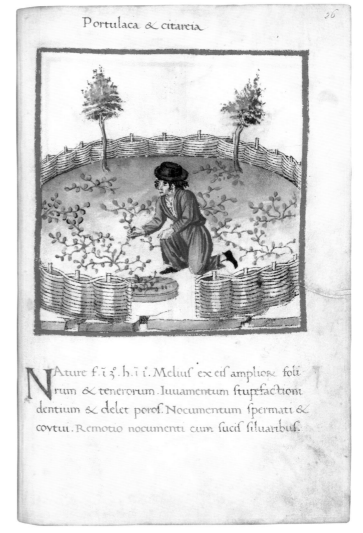

NAture f. ī ꝫ. h. ī i̇. Meluf ex eif amplio⸗ foli
rum & tenerorum. Iuuamentum ftupefaction
dentium & delet porof. Nocumentum fpermati &
covtui. Remotio nocumenti cum fucif filuaribuf.

Fig. 11 Fig, from the Rouen *Tacuinum. Rouen, Bib. Mun., MS 3054, f. 1v*

Fig. 12 Purslane, from the Rouen *Tacuinum. Rouen, Bib. Mun., MS 3054, f. 26r*

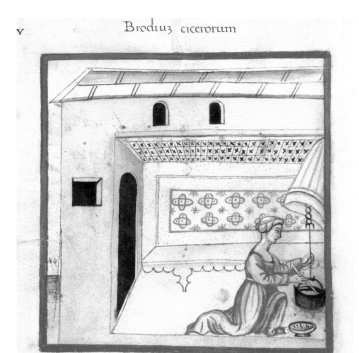

Brodiuz cicerorum

v

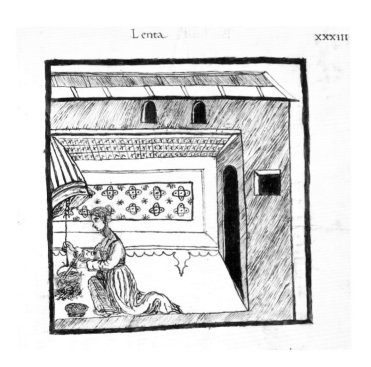

Lenta

XXXIII

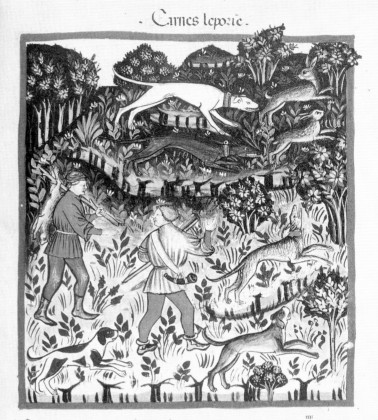

· Carnes lepozie ·

Carnes lepozie. 2plo. ca. stc mr. Electo. Iuniores capti. puenatores canes. uua. resunt supa-
tis amulta pinguedie. Nocumtum uigilar fatuir. Kemo noumm ei apoma arowuatibus.
uliatuus. Quio quanr humore melecolicu. sueuint mag. fris xerepitis. breme z. fris re-
gionibz

top left
Fig. 13 A woman stirs a pot of chickpea broth. *Liechtenstein* Tacuinum,
p. XXXIV (no. 47)

bottom left
Fig. 14 This illustration for lentils is traced from the illustration on the opposite side of the leaf. *Liechtenstein* Tacuinum, *p. XXXIII (no. 46)*

right
Fig. 15 Hare meat, from the Vienna *Tacuinum*: compare with no. 64. *Vienna,
ÖNB, cod. ser. nova 2644, f. 72r*

manuscript was written in Venice or Padua and illuminated in Venice in 1458–59.[44] The patronage and illumination of the Albi Strabo allows us circumstantially to locate its scribe to the Veneto – perhaps even to Padua – and associates him with patrons and artists of distinction.

Other manuscripts attributed by de la Mare to the Albi Strabo scribe are listed on p. 46. The pattern of production revealed by this list shows that he worked principally in the Veneto, with much of his work associated with Verona, Venice and especially Padua. Active from the late 1450s to the late 1460s, the Albi Strabo scribe undertook commissions from powerful patrons such as the aforementioned Venetian Jacopo Antonio Marcello, Janos Vitéz, Archbishop of Esztergom from 1465 (Paris, Bnf, lat. 7803; Vatican, Pal. Lat. 1711; and Vienna, ÖNB, cod. 644), and Ermolao Barbaro, Bishop of Verona from 1453 to 1471 (Vienna, ÖNB, cod. 2152). On the basis of the Albi Strabo scribe, then, we can be fairly sure that the Liechtenstein-Rouen *Tacuinum Sanitatis* was also copied in the Veneto, probably in the 1450s.

How might the Liechtenstein-Rouen *Tacuinum* fit within this context? Clearly, such an ambitious project could only have been undertaken by a wealthy patron connected to the humanist circle that included the Albi Strabo scribe. Perhaps the *Tacuinum* appealed to these humanists because of the ancient medical knowledge it contained as well as for its delightful images of contemporary life. It could have been an extravagant gift of the sort that, as we have already seen, was often exchanged within the circle of friends around Marcello. Marcello's bibliographic gifts to René of Anjou, for example, included not only the Albi Strabo in 1458–59 but also a *Passion of St Maurice* in 1452–53 (Paris, Bibliothèque de l'Arsenal, MS 940) and a copy of Ptolemy's *Cosmographia* in 1457 (Paris, Bnf, lat. 17425).[45] Perhaps the Liechtenstein-Rouen *Tacuinum* was commissioned for or by Marcello or King René, as an expression of their mutual interest in classical texts.

Since the Albi Strabo scribe was based in the Veneto, the Liechtenstein-Rouen *Tacuinum*'s four illuminators were probably also based there. There is further reason to think that this team may have been based in Padua.[46] The style of the Liechtenstein-Rouen *Tacuinum* has striking formal similarities with the famous Picture Bible made in Padua in the 1390s [fig. 22].[47] The Paduan Picture Bible is illustrated with drawings washed in colour in a technique analogous to that of the Liechtenstein-Rouen *Tacuinum*. The Picture Bible miniatures are framed, like those of the *Tacuinum*, with a simple scarlet border, and many of its scenes are set in domestic interiors, cut away to reveal the action inside. If the Picture Bible establishes a formal precedent for the *Tacuinum*, the importance of Padua as a centre for the production of illustrated Herbals is equally significant.[48] The most celebrated of these is the Carrara Herbal, made for Francesco Carrara the Younger in Padua between 1390 and 1404.[49] The illustration for basil in the Carrara Herbal, showing the plant growing standard in an elegant vase [fig. 8], is remarkably similar to that of the Liechtenstein-Rouen *Tacuinum* (no. 9), suggesting that they shared a common iconographic source. Three strands of evidence – the style of the Paduan Bible, the tradition of Herbal production in Padua, and the connection between the Albi Strabo scribe and Padua – together strongly suggest that the Liechtenstein-Rouen *Tacuinum* was also made in Padua.

Illustrating the Good Life

The 130 miniatures of the Liechtenstein *Tacuinum* offer a window into the diet, activities and lifestyle of an affluent Italian household. Exotic luxuries such as camel meat (no. 67) and ambergris (no. 84) or expensive products such as theriac (no. 16), an antidote to poison, are included in the Liechtenstein *Tacuinum*, but its main emphasis falls on relatively ordinary foods. Most of the illustrations are concerned with culinary staples like pulses and grains (nos. 31–49), eggs (nos. 56–58), and meat (nos. 63–83). These images give a sense of the impressively varied diet available to wealthy consumers, made up of fruit, vegetables, grains, dairy products and meats, and enhanced with herbs, spices and condiments such as verjuice (no. 89) and honey (no. 97).

Images show customers buying items from butchers (*e.g.* no. 66) and merchants (*e.g.* no. 29). The many miniatures featuring shopping reinforce the idea that a healthy household depended on knowledgeable specialist merchants. But the affluent households depicted in the Liechtenstein *Tacuinum* did not obtain all their food from shops. Some delicacies, such as hare meat (no. 64), were procured by hunting, and others, such as partridge eggs (no. 58), by foraging in the wild. Equally, staples such as rye (no. 44) and spelt (no. 39) are shown being tended by labourers.

Perhaps the most remarkable series of images in the Liechtenstein *Tacuinum* concerns meat, to which twenty miniatures are devoted. This cycle of images depict fresh meats such as veal (no. 69), pork (no. 66), mutton (no. 65) and hare (no. 64), as well as methods of preparing meat, such as roasting (no. 71) and preserving (no. 70). Offal is treated with special enthusiasm, with miniatures

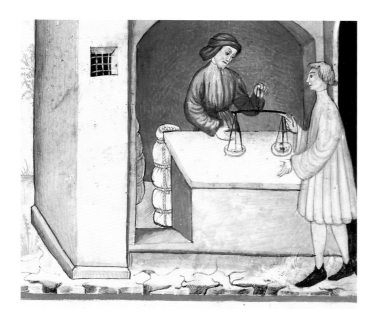

Fig. 16 A rice shop improbably situated on the edge of a cliff. *Liechtenstein Tacuinum, p. XXIX (no. 43)*

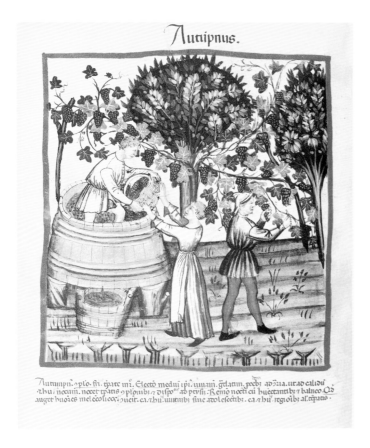

Fig 17 Autumn, from the Vienna *Tacuinum*: compare to no. 107. *Vienna, ÖNB, cod. ser. nov. 2644, f. 54v*

illustrating the preparation and consumption of delicacies such as eyes (no. 74), brains (no. 73), udders (no. 78) and rooster testicles (no. 83). While these images might suggest a degree of gastronomic adventurousness (at least to squeamish modern viewers), they also reflect a thrifty approach to household management. Nothing goes to waste in the *Tacuinum*: scraps that fall to the ground are immediately gobbled up by hungry pets [fig. 21].

Many images depict the preparation of food in domestic kitchens. Cooks stir vats of soup (*e.g.* no. 32), attend roasts (no. 71), and co-operate to make pasta (no. 38) and prepare tripe (no. 77). Other scenes show the consumption of dishes, for example couples enjoying a picnic of crayfish (no. 85) and a feast of animals' eyes (no. 74).

Food and drink are not the only factors that contribute to health: the domestic environment, the seasons and the weather are among the other subjects illustrated. Each of the seasons is represented by a miniature evoking its qualities. Spring (no. 105) shows young men and women in a rose garden, summer (no. 106) is epitomized by the harvest of crops, autumn (no. 107) by the pressing of grapes, and winter (no. 108) depicts an old man warming himself in front of a crackling fire. The iconography of these scenes draws on the analogy between the seasons of the year and the seasons of life, from the springtime of youth to the old man of winter.

Regulation of the emotions and participation in the right activities also contribute to health. The beneficial effects of conversation (no. 120), dancing (no. 126) and instruction (no. 129) are all illustrated. One miniature coyly illustrates the importance of sex (no. 124), and elsewhere the *Tacuinum* repeatedly offers advice about aphrodisiac and sperm-producing foods. Amorous couples are often shown dining on such foods, such as crayfish (no. 85) and eyes (no. 74). The importance of sleep is underlined by a series of images illustrating the soporific effects of conversation (no. 120), disorders such as sleep-talking (no. 123) and insomnia (no. 122), and sleep in its optimum form (no. 121).

Fig. 18 Purging: one of the 36 subjects in the Rouen *Tacuinum* left without an illustration. *Rouen, Bib. Mun., MS 3088, f. 51v*

Fig. 19 Detail of text for *Syrupus acetosus de citoniis* from the Rouen *Tacuinum*. The space left for the illustration was left blank. *Rouen, Bib. Mun., MS 3088, f. 45v*

The History of the Liechtenstein Tacuinum

The relationship between the two volumes of the Liechtenstein and Rouen *Tacuinum* was first revealed in the 1981 Sotheby's catalogue of the sale of Carleton R. Richmond, of Boston.[50] It might seem surprising that this connection had not been discovered sooner, especially given the amount of scholarly attention devoted to the *Tacuina*. That it took so long to recognize that the Liechtenstein and Rouen manuscripts were originally a single volume is testament to the cunning of the unknown binder who separated them. The Liechtenstein *Tacuinum* was, until recently, in binding of red morocco discreetly stamped on the inside *Belz-Niedrée*, identifying the binder as Jean-Philippe Belz (1831–1917) [fig. 23].[51] The Belz-Niedrée binding must have been added some time after this *Tacuinum* was divided into two, because (as discussed below) their separation must have taken place before 1838, when the manuscript was purchased by the Bibliothèque municipale of Rouen as part of the library of Constant Leber.

The binder who divided the Liechtenstein-Rouen *Tacuinum* disguised the relationship between the two resulting books in several ways. First, he attempted to prevent anyone from observing that either of the manuscripts was incomplete. This he accomplished by dividing the miniatures between the two volumes in such a way that both seemed to represent all of the main topics of the *Tacuinum*. So, for example, the Liechtenstein-Rouen *Tacuinum* includes illustrations of five types of wine, two of which are in Rouen while the remaining three are in the Liechtenstein volume. A different but equally crafty strategy was employed for subjects that fell neatly into sets. Splitting groups such as the four winds or the four regions would immediately have alerted the viewer that something was missing. Therefore, the binder placed all four winds in the Liechtenstein volume (nos. 109–12).

Other methods again were employed to make each volume appear complete. The Liechtenstein *Tacuinum* was paginated with Roman numerals executed in a quasi-humanist hand, aping the script of its subject headings, and a forged index was added to the end of the book in the same hand. Both of these features were surely intended to reassure the viewer that he held in his hands a complete volume, attested by a contemporary index. The Belz-Niedrée binding further confused the identification of the Liechtenstein manuscript as a *Tacuinum* by the title on its spine: *DIETA / RUSTICA / ET CIVILIS* (Rustic and civilized diet).[52] By lopping off the Liechtenstein volume's lower margin, and with it the text that it contained, the binder made the two volumes different sizes and greatly reduced the amount of the Albi Strabo's distinctive handwriting on each page. In short, he did everything he could to make the two volumes as different in scale and appearance as possible.

Qualitative criteria seem to have informed the division of the *Tacuinum*, with the better set of miniatures reserved for the Liechtenstein volume. The Liechtenstein manuscript contains 26 more subjects than the Rouen volume. In the Rouen volume 36 subjects consist of their titles alone, with the spaces intended for miniatures left blank. Furthermore, the Rouen volume consists principally of plants, with the Liechtenstein volume containing the lion's share of images of figures at work, leisure and at rest.

We do not know who charged the binder with the task of cutting the Liechtenstein-Rouen *Tacuinum* into two, but it is not hard to deduce that the motive for this deed must have been commercial. The practice of breaking up manuscripts and selling individual leaves and cuttings has a long history, arguably stretching back into the Middle Ages.[53] Sometimes this regrettable activity has had altruistic motives. Eminent collectors such as John Ruskin, for example, extolled the didactic value of manuscript cuttings: "There are literally thousands of manuscripts in the libraries of England of which a few leaves, dispersed among parish schools, would do more to educate the children of the poor men than all the catechisms that ever tortured them".[54] A similar justification was offered by the self-proclaimed 'biblioclast' Otto Ege, surely the most prolific book-breaker of the twentieth century, who assembled portfolios of cuttings and sold them to libraries and museums all over North America.[55]

Profit, however, is more usually the dominant incentive for book-breaking. The clever concealment of the relationship between the Liechtenstein and Rouen volumes makes it seem highly unlikely that the motivation for dividing the manuscript was entirely scrupulous. Coincidentally, the Liechtenstein-Rouen *Tacuinum* is not the only clandestinely broken manuscript to be associated with Belz-Niedrée. Another is the celebrated Hours of Catherine of Cleves, the two main parts of which were reunited in the collections of the Pierpont Morgan Library in 1970.[56] Like the *Tacuinum*, the constituent parts of the Catherine of Cleves Hours were rebound so that it would appear they were complete manuscripts. So successful was this ploy that it was not until 1963 that the two books were discovered to have been part of the same volume.[57] "By dividing [t]his treasure so deceptively as to make each part seem virtually complete", wrote Erwin Panofsky, "somebody was able to reap

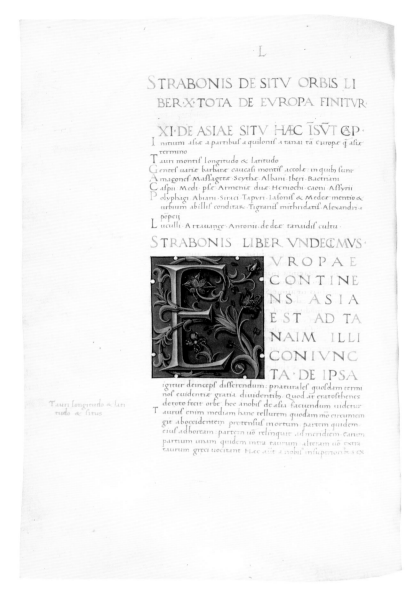

Fig. 20 Strabo's *Geography*, translated by Guarino of Verona, Venice or Padua, 1458–59. *Albi, Bib. Mun., MS 77, f. 230v*

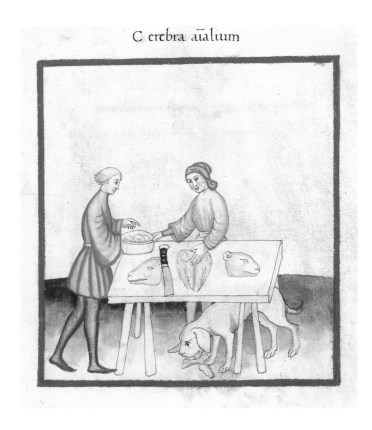

C cerebra añalium

Fig. 21 Animal brains. *Liechtenstein Tacuinum, p. LXXV (no. 73)*

facing page
Fig. 22 Craftsmen making robes and furnishings in the Paduan Picture Bible.
Padua, 1390s. *London, British Library, Add. MS 15277, f. 16r*

a double benefit for his pains."[58] This "clever but unscrupulous dealer", Panofsky speculated, might have been Jacques Joseph Techener (1802–1875), a leading Parisian merchant whose clients included ancestors of the last private owner of the section of the Hours of Catherine of Cleves acquired first by the Pierpont Morgan Library (New York, Pierpont Morgan Library, M. 917).

It is possible that the dissection of the Liechtenstein-Rouen *Tacuinum* might have had something to do with the notorious Count Guglielmo Libri (1802–1869), whose activities as a collector, dealer and thief have been well documented.[59] A precocious mathematician, Libri received a doctorate in the natural sciences from the University of Pisa in 1820, and was appointed a Professor at Pisa soon afterwards. He was, even at this early stage, already an avowed bibliophile, and was particularly fascinated with the history of science. Evidently, Libri's precocity was not confined to science and its history, for his career as a book thief also seems to have had an early start. In pursuit of his ambition to write a history of Italian science, in 1823 Libri was given unfettered access to Florence's Archivio Mediceo. In 1825 he was appointed librarian of the Accademia dei Georgofili in Florence, only to resign unexpectedly the following year. His successor discovered that more than 300 volumes were missing from the collection, but Libri's strenuous protestations averted a potential scandal.[60]

The true extent of Libri's manuscript thefts remains murky, and we will probably never be certain whether he played a role in the history of the Liechtenstein-Rouen *Tacuinum*. We know that over a long period he stole manuscripts from libraries in France and Italy, removed original evidence of their provenance and faked alternative origins, then passed them off (or tried to) as books of which he had legitimate ownership.[61] A client of the Paris dealer Techener,[62] Libri also occasionally sold volumes – sometimes of questionable provenance – through him.[63] Circumstantially, at least, the division of the Liechtenstein-Rouen *Tacuinum* fits into the time of Libri's nefarious activities and his association with Techener in the 1830s.

The smaller part of the *Tacuinum* was acquired by the historian and bibliophile Jean Michel Constant Leber (1780–1859), who sold it with the rest of his library in 1838 to the Rouen Bibliothèque municipale. Leber's catalogue of the manuscripts he sold to the Bibliothèque municipale, published in 1859, describes the *Tacuinum* in its present fragmentary state, so we can be reasonably certain that it was in this form when he acquired it.[64]

The Liechtenstein *Tacuinum* first surfaced in 1887, when it (or an

Como Beselehel e Ohab so compagno si scolpisse in le pue pretiose le nome deli dodexe fioli de Iacob.
Como Beselehel e Ohab so compagno lauora la uestimenta sacerdotale de Aaron.

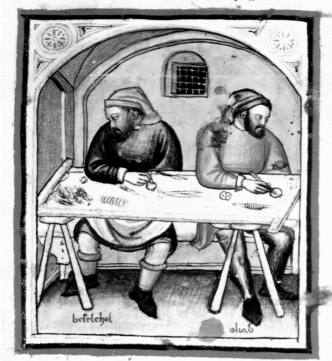

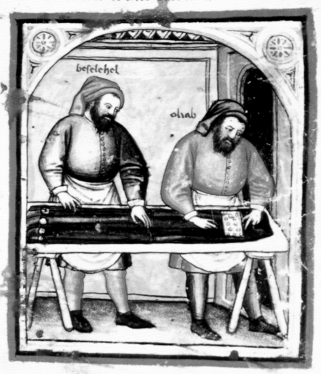

Como Beselehel e Ohab so compagno lauora el Candeliero de oro.
Como Beselehel e Ohab so compagno lauora le colone del tabernaculo.

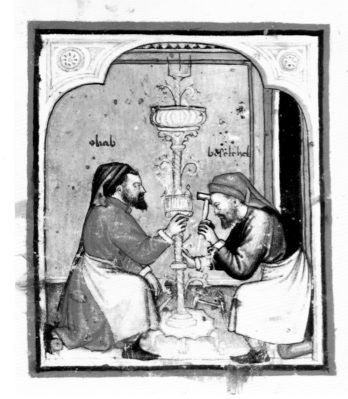

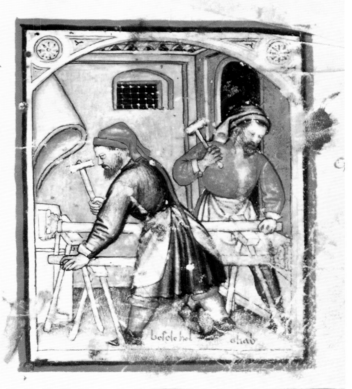

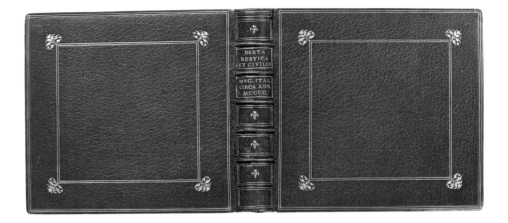

exact copy) was used by Victor Gay as the source for several plates in his *Glossaire Archéologique du Moyen Age et de la Renaissance*.[65] Christopher de Hamel has suggested that Gay himself might have owned it; if so, it may have been during this period that it was re-bound by Belz-Niedrée.[66] Before long, it entered the library of Prince Liechtenstein. In 1948, it became one of the first acquisitions that the New York bookdealer H.P. Kraus made from the Liechtenstein library. In his autobiography, Kraus describes how he purchased the *Tacuinum* along with another manuscript from Prince Franz Joseph II of Liechtenstein "as appetizers with hopes of more to come" from this extraordinary library.[67] So greatly did Kraus esteem this *Tacuinum* that he included it in his *In Retrospect*, a survey of the hundred greatest manuscripts sold during his long career published in 1979, and in 1981 he purchased it again.[68]

The Tacuinum Past and Present

The Liechtenstein-Rouen *Tacuinum* looks back over a medical tradition spanning 1500 years. In this respect, it is an expression of the Renaissance fascination with ancient learning. Its anonymous scribe, also responsible for the extraordinary Albi Strabo, was a contemporary of important humanist scribes such as Bartolomeo Sanvito and Felice Feliciano. Yet the style of this *Tacuinum*'s miniatures neither harks back to antique sources nor responds to contemporary developments in Renaissance art: instead, they refer to their late fourteenth-century antecedents for iconography and style. The Liechtenstein *Tacuinum*, then, is something of a Janus-faced book, its script looking forward to the humanist Renaissance and its images looking back to late medieval sources.

Soon after the Liechtenstein-Rouen *Tacuinum* was made, the tradition of illustrated medical manuals was dramatically transformed. As the printing press, invented in the 1450s, gradually began to overtake the production of handwritten manuscripts, the dissemination of medical knowledge accelerated. The tabular *Tacuinum* itself first appeared in print in 1531, in an edition of which many copies survive.[69] Even more significantly, the era of Galenic medicine – which had endured since Antiquity – began to wane. Some 90 years after the Liechtenstein-Rouen*Tacuinum* was made, a systematic revision of the principles of Galenic medicine was initiated with the publication of Andreas Vesalius's study of human anatomy *De humani corporis fabrica* in 1543.

The development of systematic scientific, anatomical, pharmacological and botanical knowledge overturned the theories that underpinned the *Tacuinum*, but it did not displace its content entirely. In the words of Roy Porter, "the teachings of antiquity […] still supply subterranean reservoirs of medical folklore".[70] Indeed some of the *Tacuinum*'s advice resonates today. It recommends the aphrodisiac properties of crayfish, for example, which (it turns out) are high in zinc, known to boost the sex drive. More broadly, the relationship the *Tacuinum* observes between emotional and physical health remains an important area of scientific enquiry. Equally, its emphasis on the importance of a balanced diet and exercise has echoes in many titles that occupy the upper reaches of today's bestseller lists. In much the same way that the self-help manuals of the twenty-first century will doubtless amuse and fascinate future generations, the Liechtenstein-Rouen *Tacuinum* provides a window into the beliefs, diet and lifestyle of its affluent fifteenth-century patron and owners.

1   Rouen, Bibliothèque municipale, MS 3054 (Leber 1088), and *olim* Liechtenstein collection, now London, Sam Fogg Ltd., 15d Clifford St., W1S 4JZ.

2   Lynn Thorndike and George Sarton, '*Tacuinum, taqwīm*', *Isis* 10 (1928), pp. 490–93.

3   For a succinct discussion of the four humours, see Nancy G. Siraisi, *Medieval and Early Renaissance Medicine: An Introduction to Knowledge and Practise* (Chicago, 1990), pp. 104–06.

4   For a recent overview of the translation movement, see Lawrence I. Conrad, 'The Arab-Islamic medical tradition', in *The Western Medical Tradition 800 BC to AD 1800*, ed. Lawrence I. Conrad, Michael Neve, Vivian Nutton, Roy Porter and Andrew Wear (Cambridge, 1995), pp. 93–138, esp. pp. 104–10.

5   Hunayn ibn Isḥāq (Joannitius), 'Isagoge', trans. H. P. Cholmeley, in *A Source Book in Medieval Science*, ed. Edward Grant (Cambridge, Mass., 1974), pp. 705–15.

6   *Ibid.*, p. 714.

7   For a short biography of Ibn Buṭlān and a list of his works, see Hosam Elkhadem, *Le Taqwīm al-Ṣiḥḥa (Tacuini Sanitatis) d'Ibn Buṭlān: un traité médical du XIe siècle. Histoire du texte, édition critique, traduction, commentaire* (Louvain, 1990), pp. 9–13.

8   This remark is translated in Conrad, 'The Arab-Islamic medical tradition', *The Western Medical Tradition 800 BC to AD 1800*, p. 122.

9   "*Incipit liber Tacuini translatus de arabico in latinum in curia illustrissimi regis Manfredi, scientie amatoris*": Venice, Biblioteca Marciana, MS Lat. 315.

10 Vendôme MS 233: see Elkhadem, *Le Taqwīm*, p. 43.

11 *Ibid.* For Faraguth, see Lynn Thorndike, *A History of Magic and Experimental Science During the First Thirteen Centuries of Our Era*, II (London, 1923), pp. 756–57.

12 Moly Mariotti listed 26 copies of the Latin *Tacuinum*, to which Bertiz added the Paneth Codex (New Haven, Yale University, Whitney Medical Library, MS 28, ff. 343r–84v): see Florence Moly Mariotti, 'Contribution à la connaissance des *Tacuina sanitatis* lombards', *Arte Lombarda* (1993), p. 38 n. 3, and Agnes Acolos Bertiz, 'Picturing Health: The Garden and Courtiers at Play in the Late Fourteenth-Century Illuminated Tacuinum Sanitatis', PhD thesis, University of Southern California (2003), pp. 68 and 319–20.

13 Facsimile edition: Elena Berti Toesca, *Il Tacuinum Sanitatis della Biblioteca Nazionale di Parigi* (Bergamo, 1937). See also François Avril, *Dix Siècles d'Enluminure Italienne (VIe–XVIe siècles)* (Paris, 1984), no. 86, pp. 100–01. Several further manuscript versions of illustrated *Tacuina* were made later in the fifteenth century: for a list, see Moly Mariotti, 'Contribution à la connaissance des *Tacuina sanitatis* lombards'.

14 Facsimile edition: C. Opsomer, *L'Art de vivre en santé. Images et recettes du Moyen Âge (Le* Tacuinum Sanitatis*) de la Bibliothèque de l'Université de Liège* (Liège, 1991).

15 Facsimile edition: F. Unterkircher, *Tacuinum Sanitatis in Medicina: Codex Vindobonensis series nova 2644 der Österreichen National Bibliothek*, 2 vols. (Graz, 1967); (2nd edn Paris, 1987).

16 Facsimile edition: L. Serra and S. Baglioni, *Theatrum Sanitatis: Codice 4182 della R. Biblioteca Casanatense* (Rome, 1940) and *Theatrum Sanitatis: Biblioteca Casanatense* (Barcelona, 1999).

17 The Liechtenstein-Rouen manuscript is the only pictorial *Tacuinum* of which there is no facsimile. Several colour plates of the Rouen portion are published in L. Cogliati Arano, *The Medieval Health Handbook* (New York, 1976), plates IV, V, VI, VII, XV, XVI, XVIII, XXI, although the text is cropped. Reproductions that include the text can be found in Moly Mariotti, 'Contribution à la connaissance des *Tacuina sanitatis* lombards,' pp. 32–39.

18 See L. Cogliati Arano, 'Il Tacuinum Sanitatis di Gian Galeazzo Visconti,' *Ca' de Sass* 104 (1988), pp. 42–54, and C. Opsomer, *L'Art de vivre en santé.*

19 For an overview of the scholarship concerning the patronage of the Vienna *Tacuinum*, see Cogliati Arano, *The Medieval Health Handbook*, p. 32.

20 Brucia Whitthoft, 'The Tacuinum Sanitatis: A Lombard Panorama', *Gesta* 17 (1978), p. 59.

21 For an important recent study of Herbals, see Minta Collins, *Medieval Herbals: The Illustrative Traditions* (London, 2000).

22 British Library, Egerton MS 747: see Collins, *Medieval Herbals*, pp. 239–65 and *passim*.

23 *Ibid.*, p. 26.

24 Roderici Fonseca Lusitani, *Historia Plantarum: Roma, Biblioteca Casanatense, MS 459, 'Tacuinum Sanitatis'* (Modena, 2001), a facsimile edition; see also Collins, *Medieval Herbals*, pp. 275–78.

25 *Ibid*, pp. 277–78.

26 Sale of Carleton R. Richmond of Boston, Sotheby's, New York, 30 October 1981, lot 48.

27 The pages of the Liechtenstein *Tacuinum* measure 167 x 171 mm, and those of the Rouen manuscript are 243 x 162 mm.

28 When Sam Fogg acquired the manuscript in late 2004, it was clear that its physical condition demanded the urgent attention of the conservator Helen Loveday. Over the 150 or so years since the volume had been bound, the glue that had been used had desiccated and stiffened, and was beginning to cause stresses and splitting along the 'shoulders' of its pages. A collation of the manuscript in its bound form was published in *Medieval Manuscripts and Miniatures*, Sotheby's, London, 17 December 1991, lot 50, p. 48.

29 Moly Mariotti, 'Contribution à la connaissance des *Tacuina sanitatis* lombards,' pp. 33 and 37 n. 2.

30 *Ibid.*, p. 33.

31 Although Moly Mariotti unaccountably left pp. CVII–CXI out of her attributional scheme, these miniatures are surely the work of Artist 3.

32 Indeed it is possible that the Liechtenstein-Rouen cycle of images may once have been larger: some miniatures could conceivably have gone astray when the manuscript was divided. Several entries that are present in all four of the other cycles are absent in Liechtenstein-Rouen.

33 The following discussion is reliant on Bertiz, 'Picturing Health', 'Appendix 1: Concordance Table for the Six Illuminated *Tacuinum Sanitatis* Manuscripts (Vienna, Paris, Rome, Liège, Rouen and Private Collection)', pp. 293–318, which includes many corrections to Cogliati Arano, *The Medieval Health Handbook*, pp. 145–49, and adds the Liechtenstein *Tacuinum* (Bertiz's 'Private Collection' manuscript).

34 Rouen, Bib. mun. MS Leber 3054 (1088), f. 49r.

35 Rouen, Bib. mun. MS Leber 3054 (1088), f. 44r.

36 Used especially for its bark, wood and resin, aloe wood is mentioned in the Bible: for example, it was one of the aromatic spices used to embalm Christ (John 19: 39). See also Deni Brown, *The Royal Horticultural Society Encyclopedia of Herbs and their Uses*, pp. 125–26.

37 Vienna, ÖNB, ser. nova 2644, f. 61v.

38 Bertiz, 'Picturing Health', pp. 304 n. 13 and 307 n. 19.

39 On the Lombard origins of the *Tacuinum Sanitatis*, see *Arte lombarda dai Visconti agli Sforza* (Milan, 1958), pp. 35–37, esp. nos. 78 and 81; Cogliati Arano, *The Medieval Health Handbook*, pp. 12–14; Whittoft, 'The *Tacuinum Sanitatis*: A Lombard Panorama', pp. 49–60; François Avril, *Dix Siècles d'Enluminure Italienne (VIe–XVIe siècles)*, pp. 100–01, no. 86; and *Western Manuscripts and Miniatures*, Sotheby's, 1991, lot 50, esp. p. 51.

40 A.C. de la Mare, personal correspondence, 9 December 1986.

41 J.J.G. Alexander and A.C. de la Mare, *The Italian Manuscripts in the Library of Major J.R. Abbey* (London, 1969), pp. 97–98, no. 36, pls XLIII–XLIV.

42 Albi, Bibliothèque municipale, MS 77.

43 Millard Meiss, *Andrea Mantegna as Illuminator: An Episode in Renaissance Art, Humanism and Diplomacy* (New York, 1957), p. 34.

44 J.J.G. Alexander, ed., *The Painted Page: Italian Renaissance Book Illumination 1450–1550* (London, 1994), pp. 87–90, no. 29.

45 Giordana Mariani Canova, 'The Italian Renaissance Miniature', in *The Painted Page*, p. 25.

46 Localization of the manuscript to Padua was suggested in *Western Manuscripts and Miniatures*, Sotheby's, 1991, lot 50.

47 Rovigo, Biblioteca dell'Accademia dei Concordi, MS 212, and London, British Library, Add. MS 15277. See *La Miniatura a Padova dal Medioevo al Settecento* (Padua, 1999), nos. 58–59.

48 Collins, *Medieval Herbals*, , pp. 279–81.

49 London, British Library, Egerton MS 2020. See F.A. Baumann, *Das Erbario Carrarese* (Berne, 1974) and Collins, *Medieval Herbals*, pp. 279–81 and *passim*; Collins erroneously gives the Carrara Herbal's manuscript number as Sloane MS 2020.

50 Sotheby's, New York, 30 October 1981, lot 48.

51 For examples of Belz-Niedrée's work, see Gustav Brunet, *La Reliure ancienne et moderne: Recueil de 116 planches* (Paris, 1878), pls. 45 and 47.

52 The spine title in its entirety reads: *DIETA / RUSTICA / ET CIVILIS. / MSC. ITAL. / CIRCA ANN. MCCCC.*

53 For the history of the trade in manuscript leaves and cuttings see Roger S. Wieck, 'Folia Fugitiva: The Pursuit of the Illuminated Manuscript Leaf', *The Journal of the Walters Art Gallery* 54 (1996), pp. 233–54; Christopher de Hamel, *Cutting Up Manuscripts for Pleasure and Profit, The 1995 Sol. M. Malkin Lecture in Bibliography* (Charlottesville, 1996); also Sandra Hindman *et al.*, *Manuscript Illumination in the Modern Age: Recovery and Reconstruction* (Evanston, Illinois, 2001).

54 Quoted by Wieck, 'Folia Fugitiva', p. 48.

55 For Ege, see Wieck, 'Folia Fugitiva', pp. 248–49, and de Hamel, *Cutting Up Manuscripts*, pp. 16–18. For a list of the whereabouts of Ege's portfolios and descriptions of the Ege collection at Boulder, see Julia Boffey and A.S.G. Edwards, *Medieval Manuscripts in the Norlin Library and the Department of Fine Arts at the University of Colorado at Boulder: A Summary Catalogue* (Fairview, North Carolina, 2002), pp. 37–55. Christopher de Hamel describes the astonishing profits that can accrue from book-breaking in *Cutting Up Manuscripts for Pleasure and Profit*, and, alarmingly, there is much evidence that the practice continues today. See, for example, an account of a Breviary dismembered in 2003: *AMARC Newsletter* 42 (2004), pp. 9–10.

56 New York, Pierpont Morgan Library, MS M. 945 and M. 917. For a recent discussion of the manuscript, with a bibliography, see *The Golden Age of Dutch Manuscript Painting* (New York, 1990), nos. 45–46.

57 For an account of this discovery see John Plummer, *The Book of Hours of Catherine of Cleves* (New York, 1964), esp. p. 11, and John Plummer, *The Hours of Catherine of Cleves: Introduction and Commentaries* (London, 1966), pp. 9–12.

58 Erwin Panofsky, in John Plummer, ed., *The Book of Hours of Catherine of Cleves* (New York, 1964), p. 11.

59 See especially A.N.L. Munby, 'The Earl and the Thief: Lord Ashburnham and Count Libri', *Harvard Library Bulletin* 17 (1969), pp. 5–21, and 'The Triumph of Delisle; A Sequel to 'The Earl and the Thief'', *Harvard Library Bulletin* 17 (1969), pp. 279–90, repr. in A.N.L. Munby, *Essays and Papers*, ed. N. Barker (London, 1977), pp. 175–92 and 193–206. For a recent biography of Libri, together with a detailed bibliography, see P. Alessandra Maccioni Ruji and Marco Mostert, *The Life and Times of Guglielmo Libri (1802–1869), Scientist, Patriot, Scholar, Journalist and Thief: A Nineteenth-Century Story* (Hilversum, 1995).

60 *Ibid.*, pp. 62–64.

61 *Ibid.*, ch. 16, 'Thief and Forger,' esp. pp. 202–13, and Munby, 'The Earl and the Thief'.

62 Rugi and Mostert, *The Life and Times of Guglielmo Libri*, pp. 121, 161, 164–65 and *passim*.

63 *Ibid.*, p. 230.

64 M.C. Leber, *Catalogue des Livres Imprimés, Manuscrits, Estampes, Dessins et Cartes à Jouer* (Paris, 1859), p. 165, no. 1088.

65 Victor Gay, *Glossaire Archéologique du Moyen Age et de la Renaissance* (Paris, 1887), pp. 154, 169, 200 and 483.

66 *Western Manuscripts and Miniatures*, Sotheby's, 1991, p. 48.

67 H.P. Kraus, *A Rare Book Saga: The Autobiography of H.P. Kraus* (London, 1979), p. 153.

68 H.P. Kraus, *In Retrospect: A Catalogue of 100 Outstanding Manuscripts Sold in the Last Four Decades by H.P. Kraus* (London, 1979), p. 153; sale of Carleton R. Richmond of Boston, Sotheby's, New York, 1981, lot 48.

69 Ibn Buṭlān, *Tacuini Sanitatis: Albengnefit de virtutibus medicinarum & ciborum* (Strasbourg, 1531).

70 Roy Porter, *The Greatest Benefit to Mankind: A Medical History of Humanity from Antiquity to the Present* (London, 1997), p. 10.

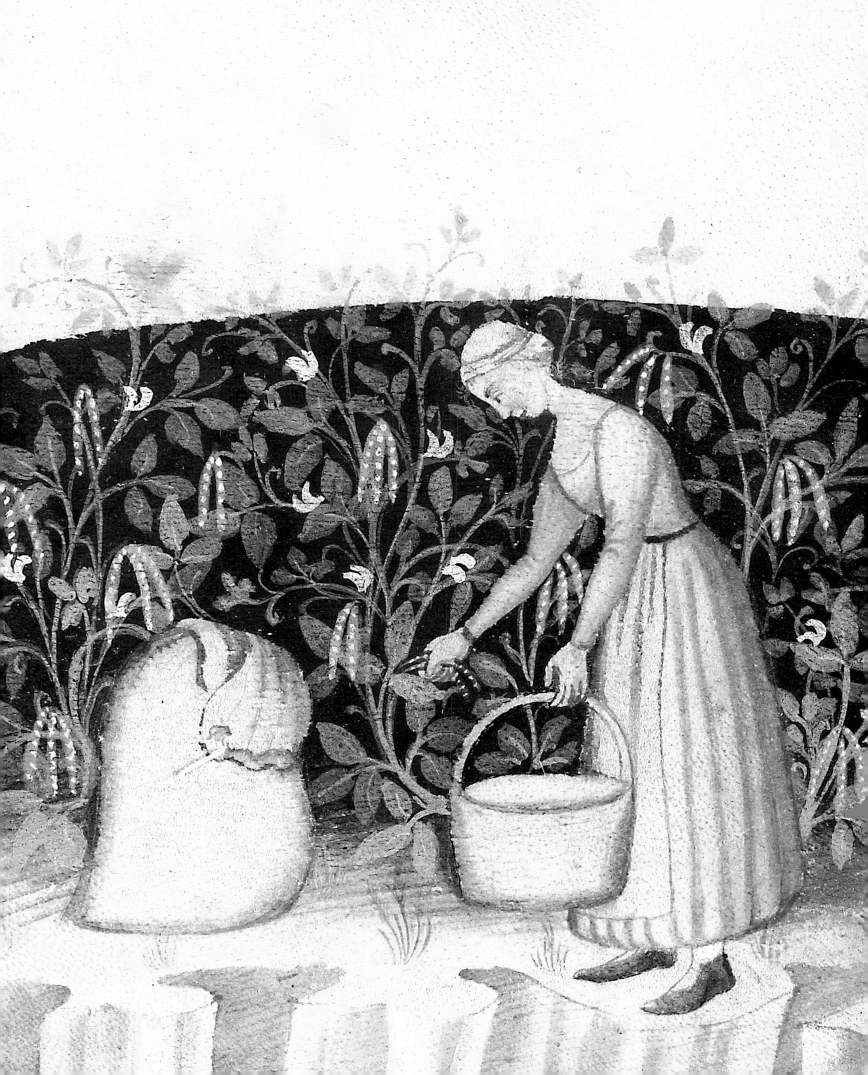

Estas

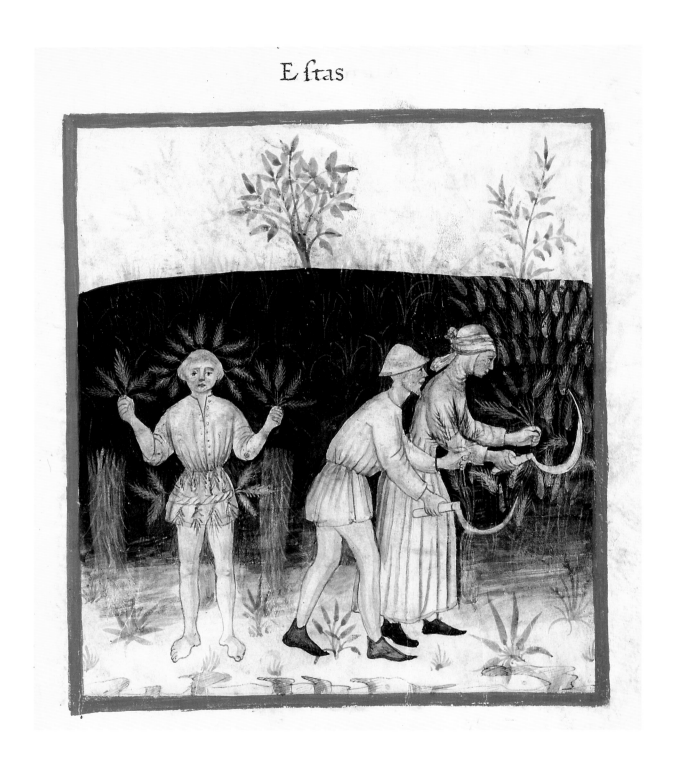

PLATE 9 **Summer**

A peasant couple mow a field with scythes. A young man stands behind them, barefoot, wearing a girdle of wheat around his head, and holding sprays of wheat in his hands: he is probably a personification of summer. *No. 106*

Spelta

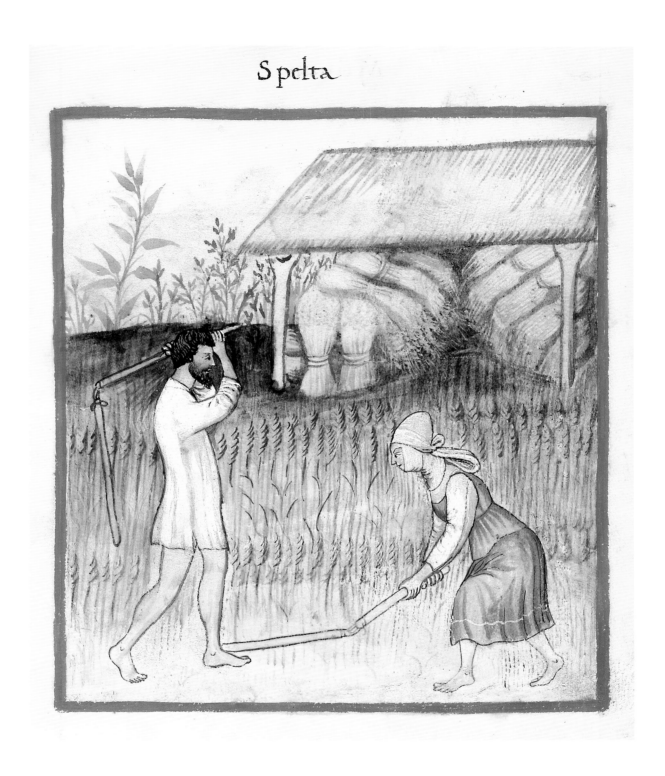

PLATE 10 **Spelt**

A barefoot peasant couple thresh spelt with flails. This scene follows the iconography of earlier *Tacuina*, adapting it for the smaller format of the Liechtenstein-Rouen manuscript. To accommodate the reduction in scale, the artist has pushed the couple dangerously close together: the woman has narrowly missed her partner's foot with her flail. *No. 39*

VER

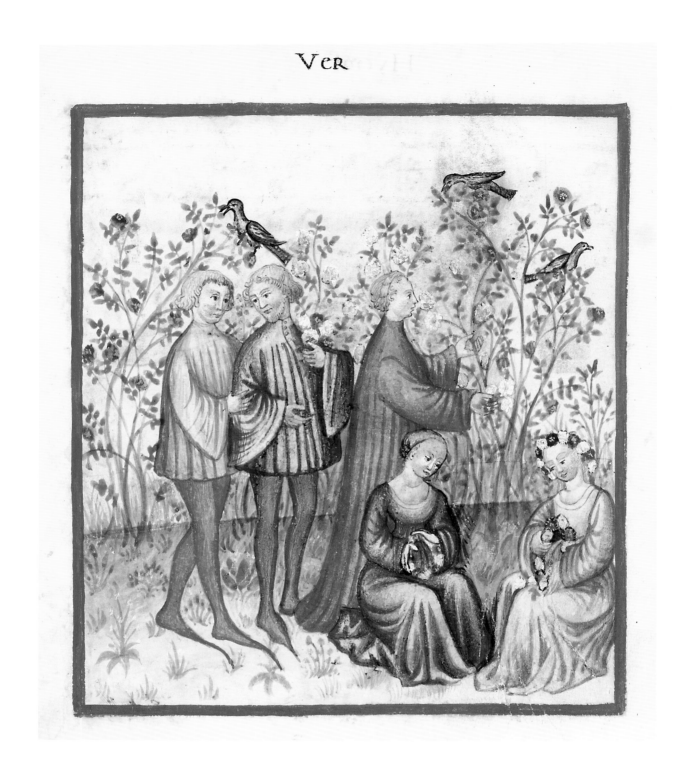

PLATE 11 Spring

A crowd of young men and women enjoy a sunny spring day in a rose garden. The women fashion garlands from the flowers, and two of the men are engrossed in conversation. *No. 105*

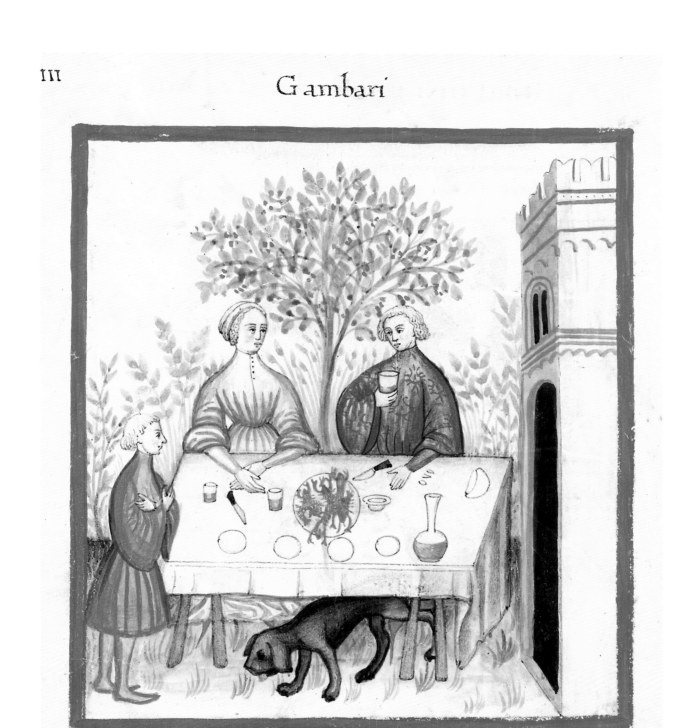

Gambari

PLATE 12 **Crayfish**

A young couple enjoy a picnic of crayfish, which is reputed to have an aphrodisiac effect. A child (perhaps a servant) looks on, as their dog snuffles under the table, searching for scraps. *No. 85*

Marubium

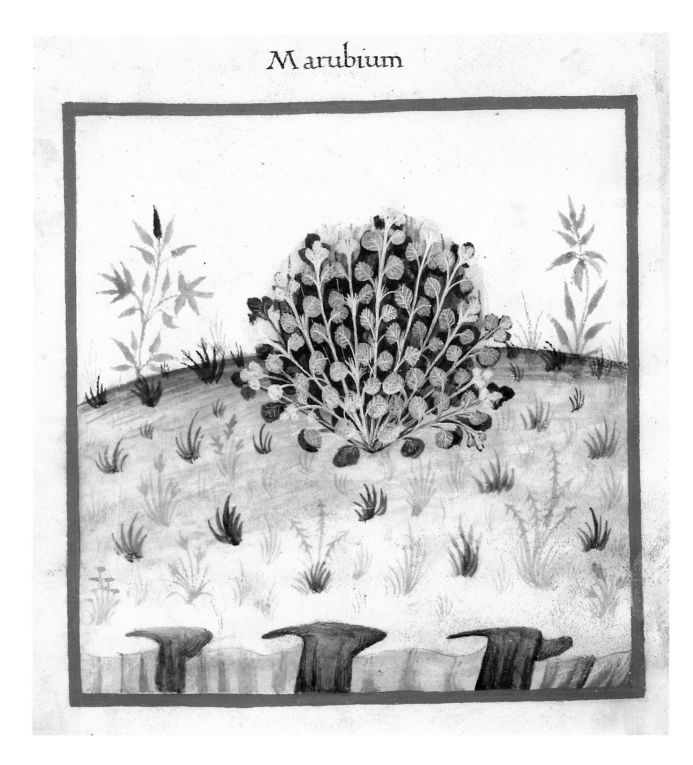

PLATE 13 Horehound

A woody horehound (*Marubium*) grows in a field. Horehound is a bitter aromatic herb, valued for its medicinal properties. *No. 2*

Viole

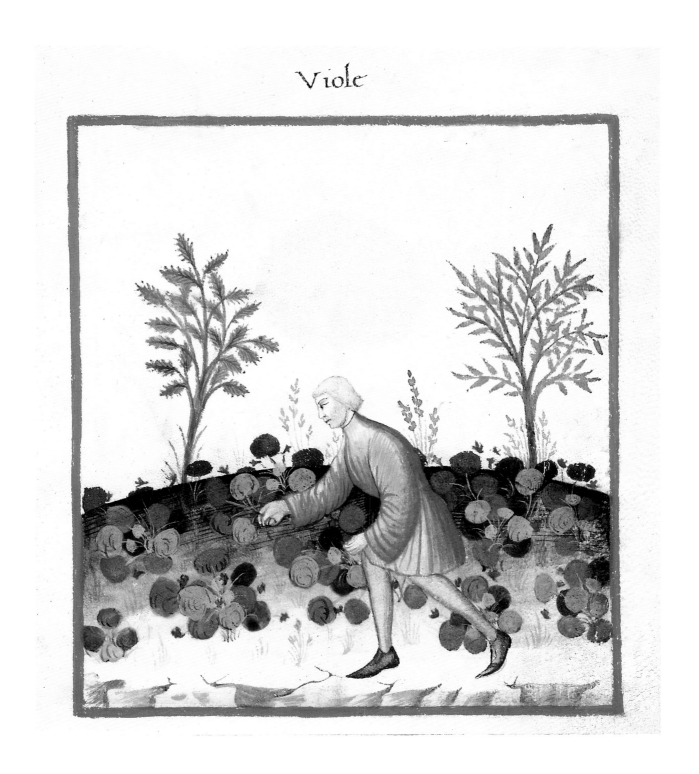

PLATE 14 **Violets**

A man stoops down to pick some violets, which are effective for calming frenzies. The best ones have flowers the colour of lapis lazuli. *No. 20*

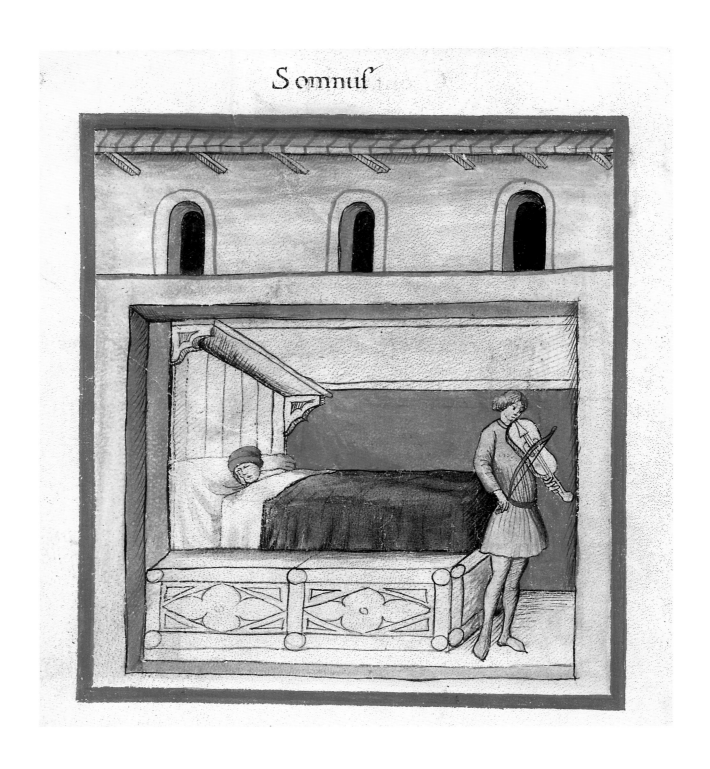

Somnuſ

PLATE 15 **Sleep**

A musician playing a viol stands at the foot of a bed, in which a man lies asleep. The *Tacuinum* recommends eight hours of sleep every night. *No. 121*

The Preface to the Liechtenstein-Rouen *Tacuinum Sanitatis*: A New Edition and Translation

CROFTON BLACK

The prefatory text of the Liechtenstein-Rouen *Tacuinum Sanitatis*, preserved in the portion of the manuscript in Rouen's Bibliothèque municipale, offers a classic example of the stylistic and terminological problems encountered by a translator working from Arabic into Latin. Like many such translations, the present example mirrors not only the meaning, but also the syntactical and structural features of the original Arabic. This results in grammatical distortion, which in turn presents difficulties in rendering the Latin into comprehensible English. Comparison with the critical edition of the Arabic text by H. Elkhadem can be of assistance. While in places the Latin represents a successful and literal rendering of the Arabic text, there can be considerable difficulty in maintaining the semantic breadth of Arabic words in Latin without resorting to paraphrase. Some terms remain intractable, and the Latin text does not match the Arabic edition with a one-to-one terminological parity.

With this in mind, in rendering the Latin text into English I have erred on the side of English fluency. Observations on the relationship between the Arabic and Latin texts are contained in the footnotes.

New edition

Tacuinu sanitatis de sex rebus que sunt necessarie cuilibet homini ad cotidianam conservationem sanitatis suae cum suis ratificationibus et operationibus. Prima est preparatio aeris qui cor attingit: secunda ratificatio cibi et potus: tertia ratificatio motus et quietis: quarta prohibitio corporis a somno et vigiliis multis: quinta ratificatio laxationis et constrictionis humorum: sexta regulatio persone in moderatione gaudii ire timoris et angustie his enim modis equalitates erunt conservatio sanitatis et remotio istorum sex ab hac equalitate facta egritudinem domini permittente glorioso et altissimo et sub quolibet horum generum sunt plures species et plurime necessarie quarum dicemus naturas. Si deo placuerit. Dicemus etiam lectiones convenientes cuilibet secundum complexionem et etatem ipsius et omnia ponemus in libro eo quod multiloquia sapientum aliquando fastidiunt auditores et diversitates multorum librorum oppositorum. Homines enim nolunt de scientiis nisi iuvamenta non probationes seu diffiniciones. Ideo intentio nostra in hoc libro est abreviare sermones prolixos et aggregare modos diversorum librorum. Attamen nostri propositi est non recedere a consiliis antiquorum medicorum.

Translation

The *Tacuinum Sanitatis* concerns the six things which are necessary for every man for the daily preservation of his health, with its regulation and its operation.[1] The first is the preparation[2] of the air which reaches the heart; the second, the regulation of food and drink; the third, the regulation of movement and rest; the fourth, the prevention of the body from excess of sleep and wakefulness; the fifth, the regulation of the loosening and thickening of the flow of humours;[3] the sixth, the regulation of the person[4] in moderation[5] of joy, anger, fear and distress. With these things being balanced there will be preservation of health, and the removal of these six things from this balance makes illness, as God glorious and most high permits.[6]

Under each of these headings are many subheadings,[7] and many necessary things, of which we will relate the natures, if it should please God. We shall also relate selections[8] which are suitable for a person in accordance with his temperament and age. We will put everything in this book,[9] because listeners[10] despise the prolixity of the wise and the diversities of many mutually disagreeing books. For men want nothing from science except for benefits; they do not want proofs or definitions. Therefore our intention in this book is to condense lengthy discourse and compile the methods[11] of diverse books. Also our intention is not to abandon the advice of ancient doctors.[12]

NOTES

1   *t'adīha* (regulation, balancing of humours), *wa-ist'imālha* (operation). The translator's use of *ratificatio*, here and below, is indicative of the terminological problems he faced. It occurs four times in the prefatory text, either to translate *t'adīha*, as here, or *taqdīr* (appointing, determining, ordaining). *Ratificatio* is not a common word in Latin and would normally be translated as 'confirmation' (see Du Cange, *Glossarium mediae et infimae latinitatis*, VII, 24). It features in legal terminology, and this perhaps accounts for its use here, as the Arabic word *'adīl* contains the idea of justice through equilibrium. The translator presumably chose it as a calque on this. For this reason I have decided to render *ratificatio* as 'regulation', although the translator also uses the word *regulatio* in this sense in one instance.

2   The Arabic reads *islah* (remedying or ameliorating).

3   The Arabic reads 'the emptying out [*istifrāgh*] and the becoming congested [*ihtiqan*] of superfluities [*fadalāt*]'. The first words are well translated by the pair *laxatio* and *constrictio*, which manage to convey the two related ideas of letting out as opposed to building up, and of free-flowing as opposed to coagulating. *Humores*, on the other hand, seems a mis-translation here; the word means 'superfluities' or sometimes 'excrements'.

4   *Persona* here substitutes *corpus* above: the Arabic is the same in each case, *nafs* (being, soul).

5   MS could also read *immoderatione, i.e.* 'from immoderation of'; I have chosen the reading which is nearer to the Arabic *bi-lqasd*.

6   The Latin syntax follows the Arabic here particularly closely. *His enim modis* translates *fī hādhā wajh* (in this manner). The translator uses *modus* later to render a different word.

7   Literally *genera* and *species*.

8   The Arabic has *ikhtiyārāt* (choices).

9   The translator has left out the reference in the Arabic text to that feature of the work which gave the *Tacuinum* its name, the table (*jadwal*). Where originally the text read 'we will put this down in a table', the Latin substitutes 'in this book'.

10   The Latin has *auditores*; the Arabic *al-nās* (people).

11   *Modos*; the Arabic has *ma'nan* (meaning).

12   The Arabic text reads that the intention is to 'follow the opinions of the ancients [*al-qudamā'*] and the moderns [*al-hadīthīn*]' alike.

Manuscripts Attributed by Albinia de la Mare to the 'Albi Strabo' Scribe

The following is a provisional list of manuscripts attributed to the Albi Strabo scribe by the late Professor Albinia de la Mare, whose research focused on Italian Renaissance scribes and book production. Some of these attributions were published under her own name in the catalogue of the manuscripts belonging to Major J.R. Abbey. Others were communicated in a letter to a previous owner of the Liechtenstein *Tacuinum*; or recorded in her notes now in the collections of the Bodleian Library; or credited to her in Lilian Armstrong's entry for the Albi Strabo in *The Painted Page* exhibition catalogue. Attributions made tentatively by Professor de la Mare are prefaced with a question mark. The sources of each attribution follow the entry.

1. Albi, Bibliothèque Municipale, MS 77: Strabo, *Geography*, translated by Guarino of Verona. Written in 1458–59 in Venice or Padua for Jacopo Antonio Marcello, the Governor of Padua, and presented by him to King René of Anjou
> J.J.G. Alexander and A.C. de la Mare, *The Italian Manuscripts in the Library of Major J.R. Abbey* (London, 1969), p. 97; Millard Meiss, *Andrea Mantegna as Illuminator: An Episode in Renaissance Art, Humanism and Diplomacy* (New York, 1957), pp. 33–34; A.C. de la Mare, personal correspondence, 9 December 1986; and Lilian Armstrong in *The Painted Page: Italian Renaissance Book Illumination 1450–1550*, ed. J.J.G. Alexander (London and New York, 1994), nos. 29, 87–90

2. London, British Library, Add. MS 24072: Matteo Bossi, *Carmina*, dated 1458
> A.C. de la Mare, personal correspondence, 9 December 1986; *Western Manuscripts and Miniatures*, Sotheby's, London, 17 December 1991, lot 50, p. 51

3. Vienna, ÖNB, cod. 2152: Donato Belloria, *De Bello Turcorum Responsio*. Dated 1460 and dedicated to Ermolao Barbaro, Bishop of Verona between 1453 and 1471
> Alexander and de la Mare, *The Italian Manuscripts in the Library of Major J.R. Abbey*, p. 97, and A.C. de la Mare, personal correspondence, 9 December 1986

4. Rouen, Bibliothèque municipale, MS 3054 (Leber 1088) and *olim* Liechtenstein, now London, Sam Fogg: *Tacuinum Sanitatis*, 1450s
> The papers of A.C. de la Mare, Oxford, Bodleian Library, and *Western Manuscripts and Miniatures*, Sotheby's, London, 17 December 1991, lot 50, pp. 48–65

5. Glasgow, University Library, Hunter MS 201 (U.1.5): Consolation to Jacopo Antonio Marcello on the death of his son Valerio by Nicolaus Secundinus, Bishop of Morviedro, and others. Shortly after 1463
> *The Painted Page*, p. 90

6. Collection of Major J.R. Abbey, JA. 3202: Leonardo Bruni, *History of Florence in nine books*, possibly made for Palla Strozzi. Probably Padua, before 1466
> Alexander and de la Mare, *The Italian Manuscripts in the Library of Major J.R. Abbey*, p. 97; A.C. de la Mare, personal correspondence, 9 December 1986; Papers of A.C. de la Mare, Oxford, Bodleian Library. Sold at Sotheby's, 4 June 1974, lot 2926

7. Paris, BnF, Latin MS 7803. Written for Janos Vitéz, Archbishop of Esztergom. Padua or Venice, *c.* 1465–70
> *The Painted Page*, p. 90, and the papers of A.C. de la Mare, Oxford, Bodleian Library

8. Vatican, Pal. Lat. MS. 1711. Written for Janos Vitéz, Archbishop of Esztergom. Padua or Venice, *c.* 1465–70
> The papers of A.C. de la Mare, Oxford, Bodleian Library, and *Western Manuscripts and Miniatures*, Sotheby's, London, 17 December 1991, lot 50, pp. 48–65

9. Vienna, ÖNB, cod. 644. Written for Janos Vitéz, Archbishop of Esztergom. Padua or Venice, *c.* 1465–70
> The papers of A.C. de la Mare, Oxford, Bodleian Library, and *Western Manuscripts and Miniatures*, Sotheby's, London, 17 December 1991, lot 50, pp. 48–65

10. Modena, Bibl. Estense, cod. lat. 447: Valturius, *De re militari*, with arms of Matthias Corvinus, King of Hungary, not before 1462
> A.C. de la Mare, personal correspondence, 9 December 1986, the papers of A.C. de la Mare, Oxford, Bodleian Library, and *Western Manuscripts and Miniatures*, Sotheby's, London, 17 December 1991, lot 50, p. 51

11. Oxford, Bodleian Library, Canon. Misc. 102, ff. 37–60v and end flyleaf: *Regulae Grammaticales*
> Alexander and de la Mare, *The Italian Manuscripts in the Library of Major J.R. Abbey*, p. 97, and A.C. de la Mare, personal correspondence, 9 December 1986

12. Oxford, Magdalen College, MS Lat. 64: Servius, *Ars Grammatica*, etc. Padua (?), *c.* 1459–61
> Alexander and De la Mare, *The Italian Manuscripts in the Library of Major J.R. Abbey*, 97 and A.C. de la Mare, personal correspondence, 9 December 1986

13. ? Oxford, Bodleian Library, Canon. Ital. 47. Headings possibly by Albi Strabo scribe
> The papers of A.C. de la Mare, Oxford, Bodleian Library

14. ? Cambridge, Fitzwilliam Museum, MS J 255: Cicero, *De Senectute, Paradoxa*, etc.
> *The Painted Page*, p. 90, and the papers of A.C. de la Mare, Oxford, Bodleian Library

15. ? Oxford, Bodleian, Canon. Lat. class. 30
> The papers of A. C. de la Mare, Oxford, Bodleian Library

16. ? Oxford, Bodleian, Canon. Misc. 146
> The papers of A.C. de la Mare, Oxford, Bodleian Library

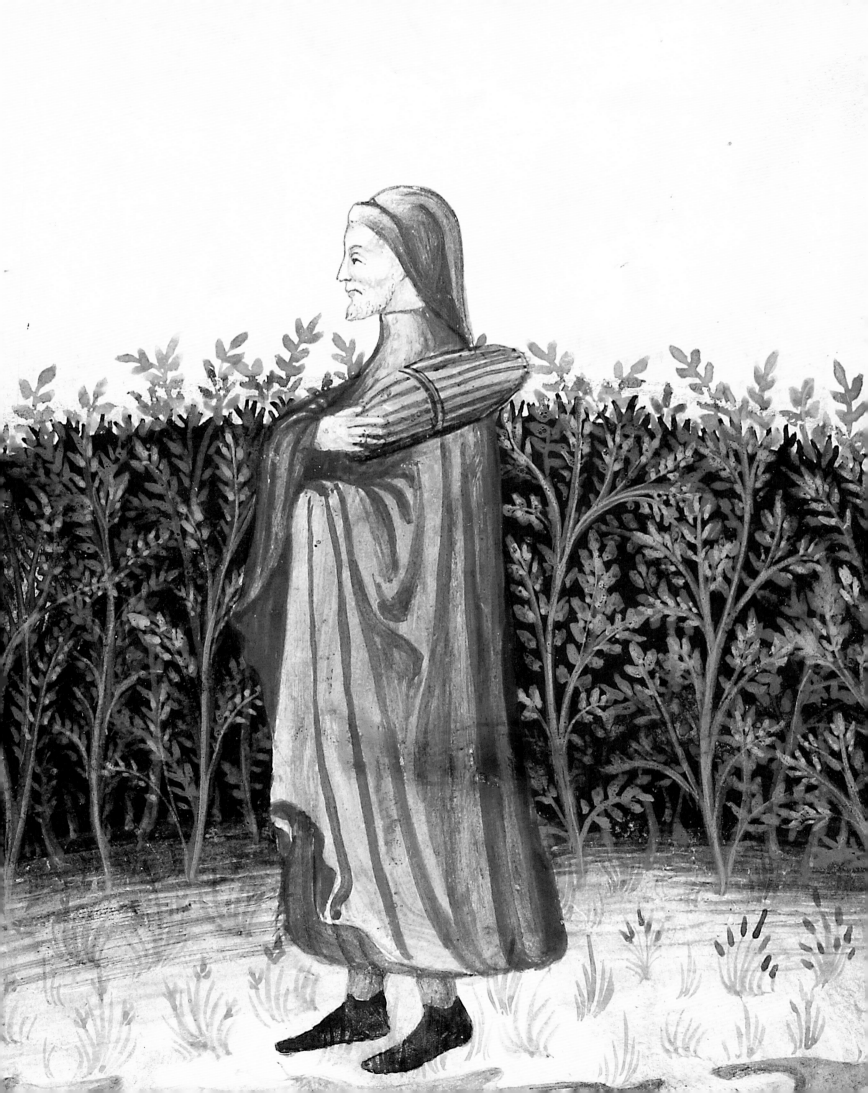

Concordance of the Liechtenstein-Rouen *Tacuinum Sanitatis*

Folios without miniatures in the Rouen manuscript are marked with an asterisk* following the folio number. Where appropriate, titles follow the Liechtenstein Tacuinum.

TITLE	ROUEN	L'STEIN	CAT./FIG.	TITLE	ROUEN	L'STEIN	CAT./FIG.
Absintium	-	III	No. 3	Carubee	f. 28v	-	
Acetum	-	XCVI	No. 90	Castanee	f. 31	-	
Adeps & pinguedo	-	LXXXI	No. 80	Caules onati	f. 20	-	
Aer epidimicus	f. 51*	-		Cefalones i dactili silvestres	f. 25v	-	
Agreste sucus	-	XCV	No. 89	Cepe	f. 22v	-	
Ale & colla	f. 36v	-		Cerebra animalium	-	LXXV	No. 72
Alea	f. 23	-		Ceresa dulcia	f. 8v	-	
Ambra	-	XCIV	No. 84	Cerosa acetosa	f. 25	-	
Amigdale amare	f. 33	-		Cetrona i narancia	f. 34v	-	
Amigdale dulces	f. 32v	-		Chorea	-	CXXXI	No. 126
Amilum	-	XXI	No. 33	Cicera	-	XXXV	No. 42
Anates & anseres	-	LXVIII	No. 60	Ciperi	-	XV	No. 11
Anetum	f. 13	-		Citra	f. 34	-	
Anguille	f. 39*	-		Coitus	-	CXXII	No. 124
Anisum	-	XVII	No. 13	Confabulationes in somnis	-	CXXI	No. 123
Apium	f. 11	-		Confabulator	-	CXIX	No. 120
Aqua caliditatis nimie	f. 43*	-		Corda animalium	-	XC	No. 82
Aqua camphore	f. 45*	-		Coria seu cutes	f. 39v*	-	
Aqua delectabilis caliditatis	f. 42*	-		Coriandrum	-	XVI	No. 12
Aqua excellentis frigiditatis	f. 41v*	-		Crocus	-	XIV	No. 21
Aqua fontium	-	CI	No. 103	Cucumeres & citruli	f. 20v	-	
Aqua frigida	f. 42v*	-		Cucurbite	f. 19v	-	
Aqua ordei	-	XXV	No. 37	Cuturnices	f. 37v*	-	
Aqua rosacea	-	CV	No. 102	Cydonia	f. 5	-	
Aqua salsa	-	CII	No. 104	Doctrina	-	CXXXII	No. 129
Armenlacha	f. 6v	-		Ebrietas	-	CXVII	No. 118
Assum in vere	f. 38v*	-		Enula	f. 16v	-	
Assum super carbones	f. 38*	-		Epata animalium	-	LXXVII	No. 75
Autumnus	-	XLVIII	No. 107	Eruca & nastrucium	f. 11v	-	
Avelane	f. 31v	-		Estas	-	XLVII	No. 106
Avena	-	XXXI	No. 45	Exercitium leve	f. 50*	-	
Avicule parve & cucardi	f. 52*	-		Exercitium moderatum cum pila	f. 49v*	-	
Bache lauri	f. 32	-		Faba	-	XXXVI	No. 24
Balneum	f. 41*	-		Faxioli	-	XL	No. 49
Baxilicum gariofolatum	-	XIII	No. 9	Feniculus	-	XVIII	No. 14
Bistarde	f. 37*	-		Festuce in aliis fistici	-	XXXII	No. 23
Blete	f. 24v	-		Fichus	f. 1v	-	
Brodium cicerorum	-	XXXIV	No. 47	Ficus sicce	-	LII	No. 30
Busuri i dactili cum incipiunt dulcescere	f. 27	-		Foca ordeaceum i al cervisia	f. 48v*	-	
Butirum	-	LIX	No. 52	Fructus mandragore	-	XIII	No. 10
Camere estivales	-	CXIII	No. 113	Furmentum elixum	-	XLV	No. 34
Camere & aer ipsius	f. 50v*	-		Furmentum	-	XX	No. 31
Camere hyemales	-	CXIV	No. 114	Galanga	f. 13v	-	
Camphora	-	CX	No. 17	Galine	f. 36*	-	
Cana mellis	-	CVI	No. 95	Galli	-	LXIII	No. 55
Candi	f. 44v*	-		Gambari	-	LXXXVIII	No. 85
Cantus	-	CXXV	No. 127	Gelatina	-	LXXXIII	No. 79
Caparis	f. 21v	-		Glandes	f. 29	-	
Capita animalium	-	LXXXIV	No. 72	Granata acetosa	f. 4v	-	
Cargagelarum & capriolorum	-	LXX	No. 63	Granata dulcia	f. 4	-	
Carnes arietum	-	LXXII	No. 65	Hyems	-	XLIX	No. 108
Carnes caprarum & proprie edorum	-	LXXXV	No. 68	Intestina id est busecha	-	LXXXII	No. 77
Carnes leporine	-	LXXI	No. 64	Ira	-	CXVI	No. 115
Carnes porcine	-	LXXIX	No. 66	Iuiube	f. 29v	-	
Carnes salite sicce	-	LXXIII	No. 70	Iuncata	-	LX	No. 53
Carnes sufrixe	-	LXXIV	No. 71	Lac acetosum	-	LVIII	No. 51
Carnes vacine & camelorum	-	LXXX	No. 67	Lac dulce	-	LVII	No. 50
Carnes vitulorum	-	LXXXVI	No. 69	Lactuce	f. 10	-	

TITLE	ROUEN	L'STEIN	CAT./FIG.	TITLE	ROUEN	L'STEIN	CAT./FIG.
Lamprete	-	XCIII	No. 87	Regio meridionalis	f. 53v*	-	
Lenta	-	XXXIII	No. 46	Regio occidentalis	f. 53*	-	
Levisticum	-	I	No. 1	Regio orientalis	f. 52v*	-	
Lilia	-	VIII	No. 19	Ribes	f. 33v	-	
Lintea	-	CXXIX	No. 132	Rizum	-	XXIX	No. 43
Liquiritia	-	XIX	No. 15	Rob de ribes	f. 48*	-	
Lupini	-	XLIV	No. 22	Rosmarinum	-	VI	No. 6
Maiorana	f. 14v	-		Roxe	-	VII	No. 18
Mala acetosa	f. 6	-		Ruta	f. 16	-	
Mala dulcia	f. 5v	-		Rutab i dactili maturi	f. 27v	-	
Marinum origanatum	-	IX	No. 7	Sal	-	LXII	No. 88
Marubium	-	II	No. 2	Salvia	-	IV	No. 4
Mel	-	CIX	No. 97	Sandalus albus	-	X	No. 8
Melega	-	XXXVIII	No. 48	Sartor	-	CXXVIII	No. 131
Melones dulces	f. 18	-		Savich id est pultes ordei	-	XXIV	No. 36
Melones indi et palestini	f. 19	-		Savich id est pultes tritici	-	XXII	No. 32
Melones insipidi	f. 18v	-		Scariole	f. 26v	-	
Melongiana	f. 21	-		Sicomori	f. 7	-	
Menta	f. 15	-		Siligo	-	XXX	No. 44
Mesch	-	XXXIX	No. 25	Sinapi	f. 12v	-	
Milium	-	XXVIII	No. 40	Sirupus acetosus	-	CXI	No. 91
Mirtus	-	V	No. 5	Somnus	-	CXX	No. 121
Muschus	-	CVIII	No. 94	Sparagus	f. 23v	-	
Muse	f. 17v	-		Spelta	-	XXVII	No. 39
Mustum	-	XCVII	No. 98	Sperma	f. 49*	-	
Nabach id est cedrum	f. 8	-		Spinachie	f. 24	-	
Napones	-	XLIII	No. 28	Splenes	-	LXXVIII	No. 76
Nespula	f. 7v	-		Sponsa	-	CXXVI	No. 117
Nuces	f. 30	-		Syrupus acetosus de citoniis	f. 45v*	-	
Nux indie	f. 28	-		Syrupus de citoniis	f. 46*	-	
Oculi animalium	-	LXXVI	No. 74	Syrupus de papaveribus	f. 46v*	-	
Oleum amigdalarum	-	CIII	No. 92	Syrupus de rosatius	f. 47*	-	
Oleum olive	-	CIV	No. 93	Syrupus iulep confectus cum aqua rosata	f. 47v*	-	
Oleum violaceum	f. 43v*	-		Tarcon i herba piretri	f. 10v	-	
Olive nigre	f. 30v	-		Terratufule	f. 9v	-	
Ordeum	-	XXIII	No. 35	Testiculi	-	XCII	No. 83
Organizare cantu et pulsare	-	CXXIV	No. 128	Tiriacha	-	XLVI	No. 16
Ova anserum	-	LXV	No. 57	Tri	-	XXVI	No. 38
Ova galinacea	-	LXIV	No. 56	Turde	-	CXXX	No. 62
Ova perdicum	-	LXVI	No. 58	Turtures	-	LXXVII	No. 59
Ozimum citratum	f. 12	-		Ubera	-	XCI	No. 78
Panicum	-	XXXVII	No. 41	Uve	f. 2	-	
Panis de fumo vel fuculis	f. 35*	-		Venatio terrestris	-	CXII	No. 125
Panis rizon	f. 35v	-		Ventus meridionalis	-	LV	No. 112
Panni	-	CXXVII	No. 130	Ventus ocidentalis	-	LIV	No. 110
Passule	-	LI	No. 29	Ventus orientalis	-	LIII	No. 109
Pastinace	f. 9	-		Ventus septentrionalis	-	LVI	No. 111
Pavones	-	LXIX	No. 61	Ver	-	L	No. 105
Pedes & tibie	-	LXXXIX	No. 81	Verecondia	-	CXV	No. 116
Persicha	f. 2v	-		Vigilie	-	CXXIII	No. 122
Petrosilium	f. 15v	-		Vinum citrinum	-	C	No. 101
Pinee	f. 17	-		Vinum de dactilis	f. 40v*	-	
Pira	f. 3v	-		Vinum incipiens fieri acetosum	f. 40*	-	
Pisces frixi infusi in herbis …	-	LXXXVII	No. 86	Vinum rubeum grossum	-	XCIX	No. 100
Porri	f. 22	-		Vinum vetus odoriferum	-	XCVIII	No. 99
Portulaca & citareia	f. 26	-		Viole	-	XI	No. 20
Pruna	f. 3	-		Vomitus	-	CXVIII	No. 119
Purgatio	f. 51v*	-		Xilo aloes	f. 44*	-	
Rafani	-	XLI	No. 26	Ysopus	f. 14	-	
Rape	-	XLII	No. 27	Zucharum	-	CVII	No. 96
Recocta	-	LXI	No. 54				

Rape

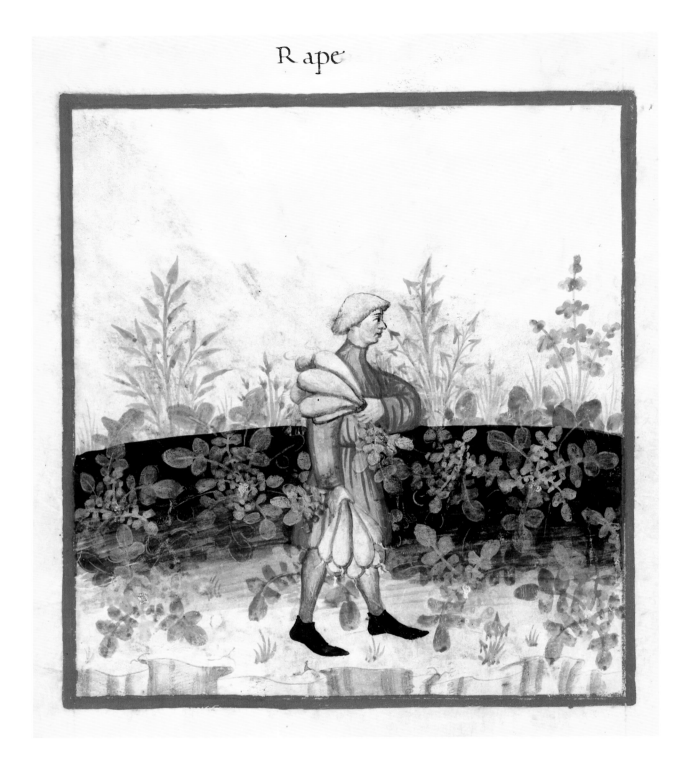

PLATE 16 **Turnips**

A man carries two fat bunches of turnips, which are recommended for myriad complaints, including poor eyesight and low sex drive. *No. 27*

Catalogue

In the following catalogue,
miniatures are arranged according to their subject:

Each entry includes a translation of the subject, followed by the page number (in Roman numerals) and a transcription of the title. Notes on the effectiveness of each subject reflect the advice provided by the other pictorial *Tacuinum Sanitatis* manuscripts.

Subjects unique to the Liechtenstein *Tacuinum* are marked with an asterisk*. Cross-references to other subjects refer to their catalogue numbers.

The sources consulted in preparing this catalogue include Cogliati Arano, *The Medieval Health Handbook,* and the facsimile editions of the Paris, Vienna and Rome *Tacuina*. See further 'Select Bibliography' on p. 76. Botanical information is principally derived from Deni Brown, *The Royal Horticultural Encyclopedia of Herbs and their Uses* (revised edn London, 2002), and Christopher Brickell, ed., *The Royal Horticultural Society Encyclopedia of Plants and Flowers* (3rd edn, London, 1999).

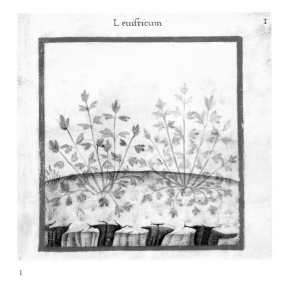

Leuisticum   I

1

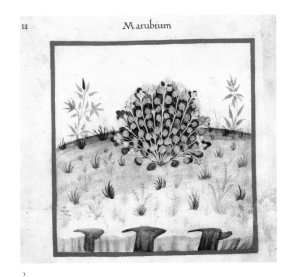

II   Marubium

2

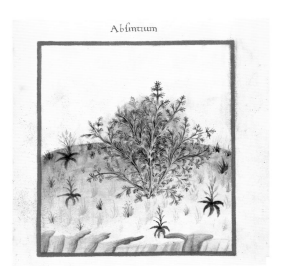

Absintium

3

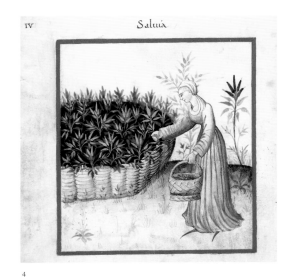

IV   Saluia

4

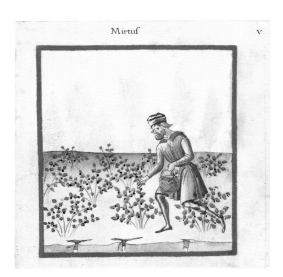

Mirtus   V

5

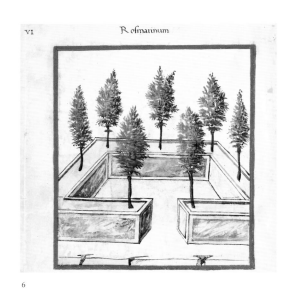

VI   Rosmarinum

6

Herbs

1 Lovage
I Levisticum
Two clumps of lovage, which is diuretic and good for killing young boys' parasitic worms.

2 Horehound
II Marubium
This illustration of a clump of horehound shows the plant's distinctive woolly foliage. Horehound generates humours and is good for the stomach and eyesight, but it can be difficult to digest. Therefore, it should be prepared with cooked must (no. 98), vinegar and other herbs. *Plate 13*

3 Wormwood
III Absintium
A shrubby wormwood. Wormwood stimulates the appetite, cures obstructions of the liver and kills parasitic worms.

4 Sage
IV Salvia
A woman gathers sage from a clump growing inside a hurdle fence. The best kind of sage is domestic, which is good for paralysis and the nerves. Its tendency to remove the colour from dark hair can be neutralized with a concoction made of myrtle and crocus.

5 Myrtle
V Mirtus
A man kneels down to pick sprigs of myrtle, an aromatic evergreen shrub. Myrtle can cause insomnia, so it is recommended that it is taken with fresh violets.

***6 Rosemary**
VI Rosmarinum
Seven rosemary bushes, trained as standards, grow in raised beds.

***7 Marine oregano**
IX Marinum origanatum
This folio was originally left un-illuminated: a later draughtsman filled in the space by crudely tracing through the miniature on the opposite side (no. 8).

*8 Sandalwood

X Sandalus albus

A man wearing a red cap kneels by a stream, fishes twigs of sandalwood from the water and places them in a shallow basin on the bank beside him. Sandalwood (*Santalum album*), indigenous to the Indian subcontinent, was prized for its fragrance and medicinal properties.

9 Basil

XII Baxilicum gar[iofolatum]

A clump of basil, trained rather improbably into a standard, grows in an elegant pot. Basil dissolves superfluities of the brain and strengthens the blood.

10 Mandrake

XIII Fructus mandragore

An anthropomorphized mandrake plant looks mournfully at a dog, whose leash is tied round the plant. This iconography reflects the ancient belief that the mandrake root, which resembled a human body, screamed when uprooted; but a dog may do the uprooting while the man goes off and thus avoids hearing its screams. In the miniature, the dog's owner turns to walk away, covering one ear with his hand. Smelled or used as a poultice, mandrake can cure headaches, insomnia, elephantiasis and other skin infections. It should not be eaten. *Plate 2*

* 11 Sedge

XV Ciperi

A young man picks fruit from a tree. The image is entitled *Ciperi*, sedges (properly *Cyperi*), these being a large family of grass-like plants used for tonics and spices. Pictured in the miniature, however, is a small grove of trees (certainly not grassy sedges) with narrow pointed leaves and small purple fruits, characteristic of olive trees.

12 Coriander

XVI Coriandrum

Three tall coriander plants in flower. Coriander cools the blood. It can be dangerous to the heart; this risk can be neutralised with vinegar syrup (no. 91).

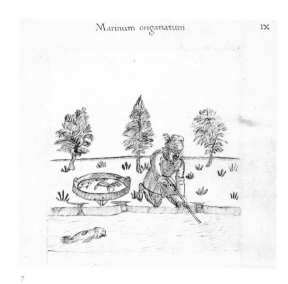

Marinum origanatum · IX

7

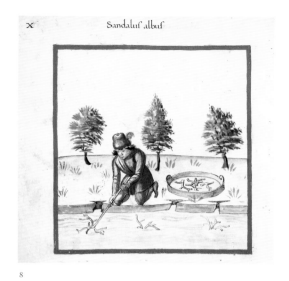

X · Sandaluf albuf

8

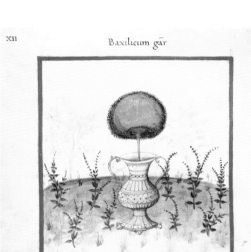

XII · Baxilicum gar

9

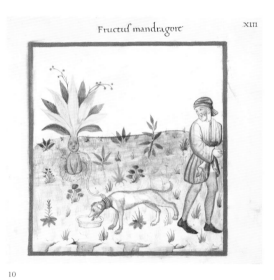

Fructuf mandragore · XIII

10

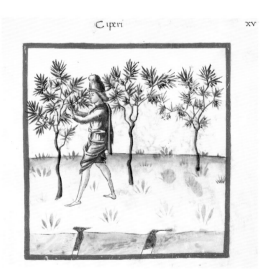

Ciperi · XV

11

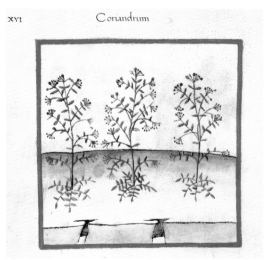

XVI · Coriandrum

12

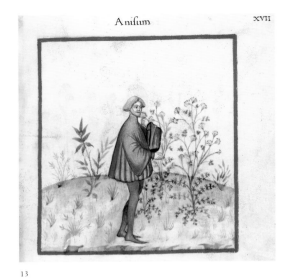

Anisum · XVII

13

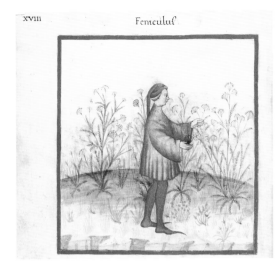

XVIII · Feniculus

14

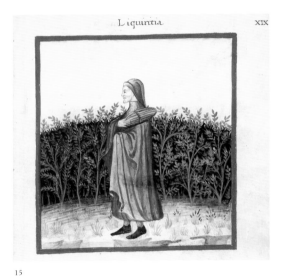

Liquiritia · XIX

15

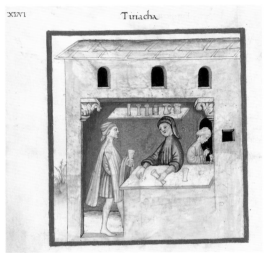

XLVI · Tiriacha

16

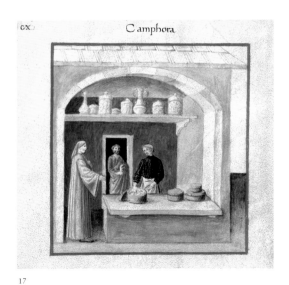

CX · Camphora

17

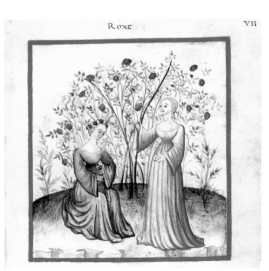

Roxe · VII

18

13 Aniseed (Pimpinella)
XVII Anisum

A man wearing a short blue tunic and parti-coloured hose sniffs a flowering sprig of aniseed. Aniseed is slow to be digested, so should be finely chopped and well chewed. It can cure hiccups and kidney stones, and is good for nursing mothers.

14 Fennel
XVIII Feniculus

A man dressed entirely in scarlet picks some fennel. The best kind of fennel is domestic, which is good for eyesight and can help to cure long fevers. It can inhibit the menstrual flow. *Plate 1*

15 Liquorice
XIX Liquiritia

A man carries a bundle of liquorice roots on his shoulder. This is most likely *Glycyrrhiza glabra*, indigenous to the Mediterranean, the roots of which were of special value. Liquorice is an appetite suppressant, and can alleviate hoarseness and constipation. It can also cause constipation, and so should be eaten with raisins.

16 Theriac
XLVI Tiriacha

An apothecary measures out grains of theriac, a valuable antidote to poison and cure for fevers and paralysis. The best kind of theriac has been aged for ten years, and will cure a rooster of the effects of poison. Theriac that is more than ten years old causes insomnia.

17 Camphor
CX Camphora

A shopkeeper opens a box of camphor, derived from the camphor tree (*Cinnamomum*) and sold as a powder, for a customer. It stops nosebleeds and remedies inflamed livers, burning eyes and fevers, but it causes insomnia. This can be remedied with the scent of violets.

Flowers

18 Roses
VII Roxe

Two ladies, one seated and the other standing, smell red and white roses flowering on bushes. The seated lady, in blue, frowns and stares at the ground, while the other reaches happily for a flower. The best roses come from Suri and Persia, and these are good for treating inflamed brains. Camphor or crocus can neutralize their tendency to cause headaches and feelings of heaviness or constriction (perhaps suffered by the woman in blue), and blockages of the sense of smell.

19 Lilies
VIII Lilia
The best lilies have blue flowers. They can help women in childbirth and dissolve superfluities of the brain, but they can cause headaches.

20 Violets
XI Viole
The best violets are the colour of lapis lazuli. Their scent can calm frenzies, and as a draught they can purify bilious humours, but they can also exacerbate catarrh caused by the cold. *Plate 14*

21 Crocus
XIV Crocus
Crocuses are the source of saffron, which is good for the heart and, soaked in raisin wine, counteracts drunkenness. It can cause nausea, against which fragrant wine (no. 99) and quince juice are effective.

22 Lupins
XLIV Lupini
A field of lupins. Lupins (*Lupinus*) have distinctive floral racemes, but interestingly these lupins are not shown in flower, thus allowing the viewer to identify the plant by its distinctive foliage alone. Lupins can thicken the blood.

Fruits and vegetables

23 Vegetables
XXXII Festuce i[n] al[iis] fistici
A woman harvests vegetables (perhaps carrots) from a tidy vegetable plot.

24 Fava beans
XXXVI Faba
A man harvests beans from a field. The best beans are red, and these are fattening and stimulate urination. They are best taken with oil, salted water and mustard.

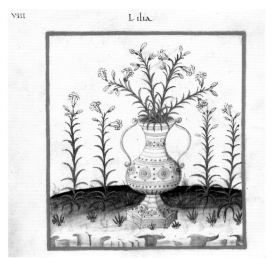

19

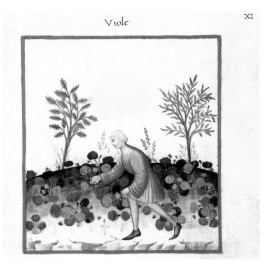

20

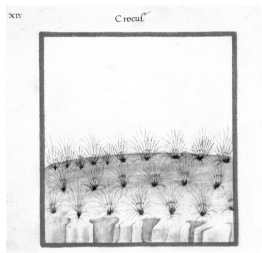

21

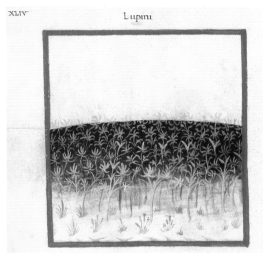

22

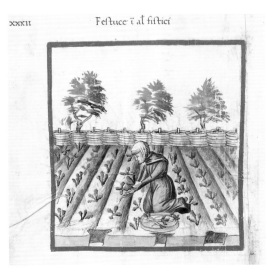

23

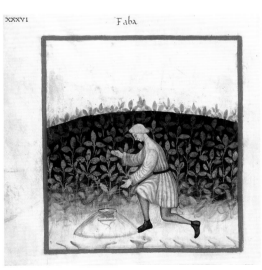

24

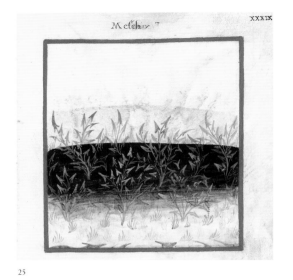

25

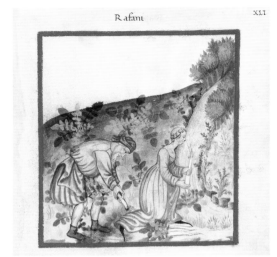

26

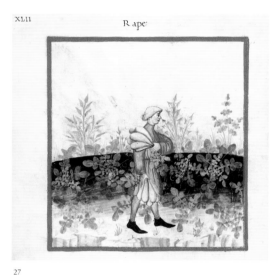

27

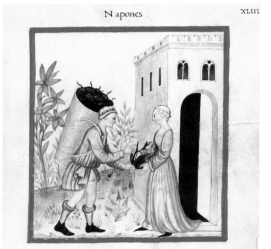

28

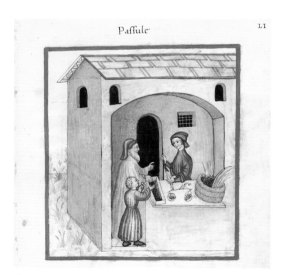

29

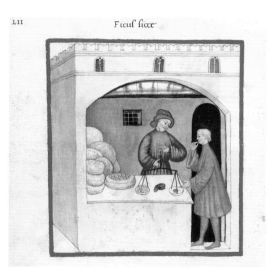

30

25 Vetchling
XXXIX Mesch

Vetchling, a type of wild pea, grows in fields. Vetchling is eaten by the poor, and only very seldom by the wealthy. It alleviates coughs and fevers, but is harmful for weak teeth and causes vertigo. It is recommended for labourers, but not for those who lead lives of leisure.

26 Radishes
XLI Rafani

A man and a woman harvest wild radishes in a hilly landscape.

27 Turnips
XLII Rape

A man carries a big bunch of turnips in each hand. The best turnips are domestic, these being thin-skinned and sweet tasting. This sort can be pickled and kept for a year. They are good for the stomach, for treating dry intestines, for eyesight and for coitus. They should be cooked for a long time, otherwise they can cause flatulence and swellings. *Plate 16*

28 Navetts; young turnips
XLIII Napones

A man, who carries a large basket of black turnips on his back, sells a few to a lady who stands outside the porch of a house. The best *napones* are long and dark, and are good for increasing sperm and reducing swellings. They can cause obstructions of the veins. To avoid this, they should be stewed twice and eaten with fatty meats.

29 Raisins
LI Passule

A child eagerly reaches towards a trough filled with raisins as the merchant and the boy's father converse. Raisins soothe intestinal pain and fortify the liver and stomach.

30 Dried figs
LII Ficus sicce

A man samples a dried fig as a merchant weighs out his purchase. Dried figs can protect against poisons, but they can also cause constipation and flatulence. They should therefore be soaked, and served with walnuts and almonds.

Grains and pulses

31 Wheat

XX Furmentum

Wheat grows in a field with purple flowers. The best wheat has large and heavy grains, which are useful for opening ulcerations. It should be well cooked, or it can cause occlusions.

32 Wheat broth

XXII Savich i[d est] pultes tritici

A woman bends down to stir a pot of wheat broth that bubbles over her kitchen fire. This nourishing soup should be made with toasted wheat, and stirred frequently as it cooks over a hot fire.

33 Starch

XXI Amilum

A merchant fills a dish with *amilum* for a female customer. This product is made from grain that has been washed repeatedly and dried in the sun. It should be white and brittle. It soothes coughs when it is prepared with almond oil (no. 92), and counteracts biliousness.

34 Boiled wheat

XLV Furmentum elixum

Two men dine at a table in a richly decorated room. A servant brings them a dish of boiled wheat. This dish should be thoroughly baked and salted, or else it can cause flatulence and many superfluities.

35 Barley

XXIII Ordeum

A field of barley. Barley is best when white, large and fresh. It is easily digested and, though it can have a beneficial laxative effect, it can cause slight pain. To avoid this, it should be toasted.

36 Barley broth

XXIV Savich i[d est] pultes ordei

Two women serve barley broth to a female invalid, who lies in bed, presumably suffering from the kind of bilious condition cured by this soup.

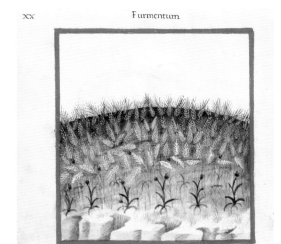

XX Furmentum

31

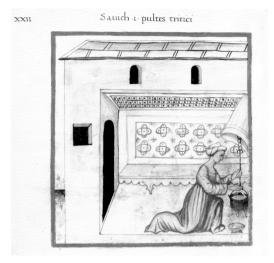

XXII Sauich i pultes tritici

32

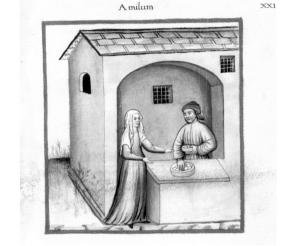

Amilum XXI

33

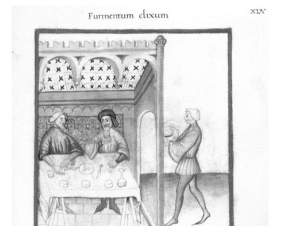

Furmentum elixum XLV

34

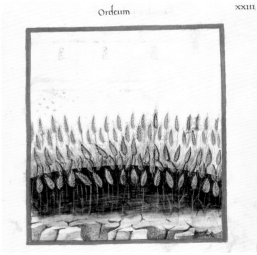

Ordeum XXIII

35

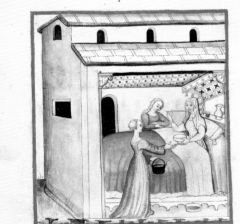

XXIV Sauich i pultes ordei

36

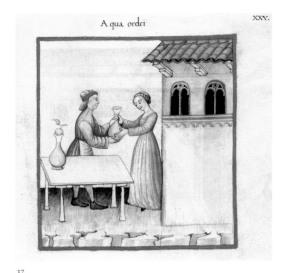

37

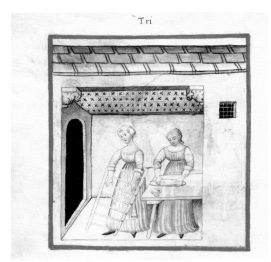

38

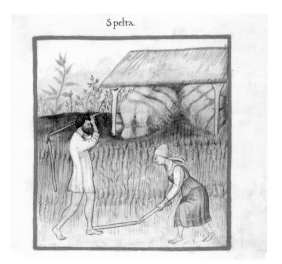

39

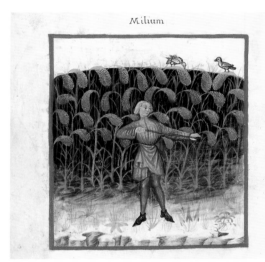

40

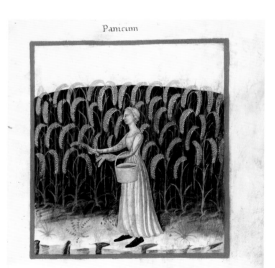

41

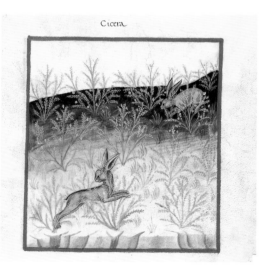

42

37 Barley water
XXV Aqua ordei
A man wearing an apron hands a bottle of barley water to a woman. This preparation should be thoroughly boiled, and is best taken with some sugar. It is useful for restoring an inflamed liver.

38 Pasta
XXVI Tri
Two women make spaghetti: one rolls out the dough, while the other sets the strands to dry on a rack. Pasta should be prepared carefully, and it is good for the chest and throat. Eat it with sweet barley to prevent it from harming the stomach and any weak intestines. It is very nourishing. *Plate 4*

39 Spelt
XXVII Spelta
A man and a woman thresh spelt in a field, with a covered barn full of bales of hay behind them. Spelt is less nourishing than wheat, and can be harmful to the stomach, but it is good for the chest and the lungs and for curing coughs. *Plate 10*

40 Millet
XXVIII Milium
Birds nibble on millet seeds, unobserved by the gentleman who stands with a stick (presumably to ward them off). Millet should be left standing in the field for three months or more. It is not very nourishing, but it is thirst-quenching, and good for the stomach. It should be cooked well, and taken with almond oil and sugar. *Plate 5*

41 Panic grass; Italian millet
XXXVII Panicum
A woman harvests panic grass, which has similar properties to millet. *Plate 6*

42 Chickpeas
XXXV Cicera
Two hares frolic in a field of chickpeas. The best chickpeas are those that are undamaged by animals or insects. They heat the blood and produce sperm, but can impair the kidneys and bladder.

43 Rice

XXIX Rizum

A merchant weighs a portion of rice for a customer. The best rice is called *margaritarum*, and preparing it with oil and milk prevents it from harming people suffering from colic. It is good for soothing an inflamed stomach.

44 Rye

XXX Siligo

A peasant mows a field of rye with a scythe. Hot from the exertion, he has rolled his hose down around his calves. Rye is difficult to digest, so should be eaten with plenty of wheat. It is useful for suppressing the sharpness of the humours.

45 Wild oats

XXXI Avena

A kneeling woman harvests wild oats. Oats have no harmful side effects.

46 Lentils

XXXIII Lenta

This miniature is one of the two left blank in the Liechtenstein *Tacuinum*: a later artist roughly traced the miniature from the reverse of the leaf, which illustrates the preparation of chickpea broth (no. 47). Lentils can soothe the stomach, but can cause melancholy, reduced sex drive and poor vision. Eat them with beets and the herb *Atriplex* (probably sea orach, also known as tree purslane).

47 Chickpea broth

XXXIV Brodium cicerorum

A woman stirs a pot of chickpea broth that cooks over the kitchen fire. This image recycles the composition used in several other miniatures, including the ones illustrating wheat broth (no. 32) and roasted meat (no. 71). This broth should be made with chickpeas, broad beans and sweet milk. It is good for treating paralysis.

48 Sorghum

XXXVIII Melega

A wild boar munches on a stalk of sorghum in a field. Sorghum is recommended for peasants and swine. It should be eaten with foods that cause merriment in order to neutralize its tendency to cause melancholy.

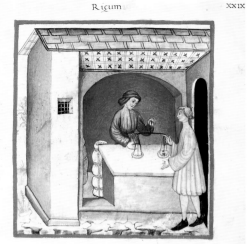

43

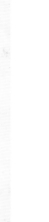

44

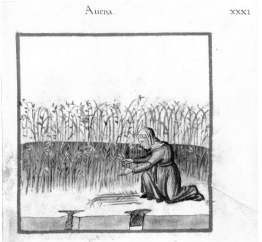

45

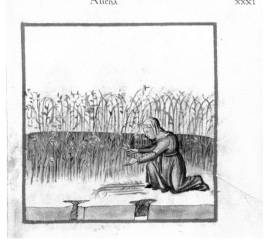

46

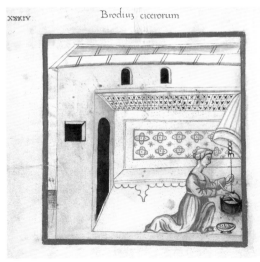

47

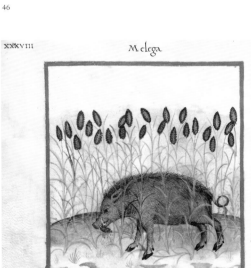

48

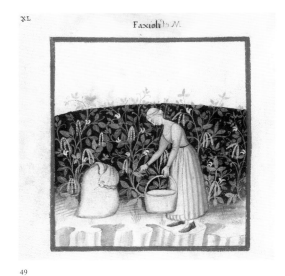

XL · Faxioli M.

49

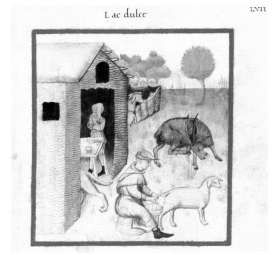

Lac dulce · LVII

50

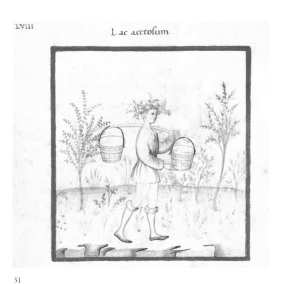

LVIII · Lac acetosum

51

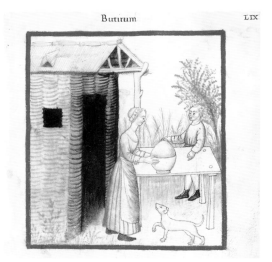

Butirum · LIX

52

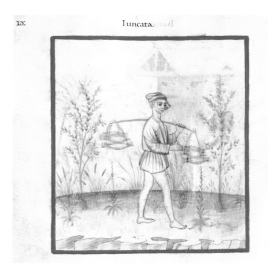

LX · Iuncata

53

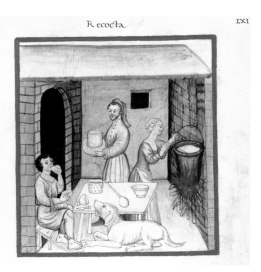

Recocta · LXI

54

49 Flax
XL Faxioli

A woman harvests flax, putting it first into her basket and then into a large sack. Flax can cause insomnia and dull the senses. To avoid this, eat it with salt and oregano.

Milk and cheese

50 Sweet milk
LVII Lac dulce

A dairy farmer milks an ewe outside his simple cottage. Inside, his son eats a husk of bread. The best milk comes from young sheep, and is good for the chest and lungs. It can cause fevers, and should therefore be eaten with seedless raisins.

51 Sour milk
LVIII Lac acetosum

A young man balances two pails of sour milk on his shoulder. Sour milk is thirst-quenching, but it can harm the teeth and gums.

52 Butter
LIX Butirum

A woman places a jar filled with butter on a table outside her house, attracting the attention of her son and dog. Butter is best when made from sheep's milk, and is useful in counteracting the superfluities in the lungs caused by coldness and dryness.

53 Junket
LX Iuncata

A young man carries bundles of fresh junket encased in reed baskets in which this fresh cheese drains. Junket should be made from the milk of young animals, and it should be eaten infrequently for breakfast with sugar and salt.

54 Ricotta
LXI Recocta

A crowded kitchen scene: a woman stirs a pot of ricotta that cooks over the fire, as a man serves bread to a beggar, who has torn hose, a rough tunic and bare feet. A large dog watches hungrily as the beggar eats. Ricotta should be made from pure milk, and is best eaten with butter and honey, which make it more digestible and prevent colic. It is nourishing and fattening. *Plate 3*

Eggs and poultry

55 Roosters
LXIII Galli

A man and woman stand by a table, presumably discussing eggs and poultry. A wicker cage of roosters and a basket of eggs rest on the table. The best roosters are those with moderate voices, which are useful for treating colic. To avoid endangering the stomach, it is advised to tire the rooster out before killing it.

56 Hen's eggs
LXIV Ova galinacea

A woman collects eggs from her henhouse with her little boy. The best eggs are large fresh ones, and these are very nourishing. Eggs stimulate the libido, but they can cause freckles. To avoid this, eat only the yolks.

57 Goose eggs
LXV Ova anserum

Goose eggs are best eaten half-cooked, and are beneficial to those engaged in heavy labour. To avoid colic, flatulence and vertigo, eat them with oregano and salt.

58 Partridge eggs
LXVI Ova perdicum

A man collects the eggs of wild partridges in the countryside. Partridge eggs are good for adolescents, convalescents and the elderly. They are best eaten when still a bit runny. They are not very nourishing, so labourers should eat them with plenty of red wine.

Birds

59 Turtledoves
LXVII Turtures

A man disguised with branches prepares to ensnare some turtledoves in his nets. Turtledoves are very nutritious, and help to cure nervous illnesses and dysentery. They are not recommended for those with melancholic temperaments, as they have a very dry meat.

60 Ducks and geese
LXVIII Anates et anseres

These birds should be rubbed with oil and filled with spices. They are good for fattening up melancholic people.
Plate 8

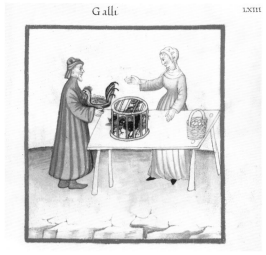

Galli · LXIII

55

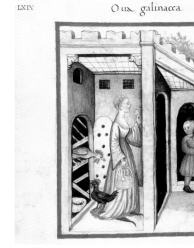

LXIV · Oua galinacea

56

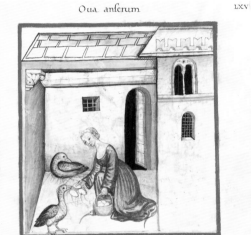

Oua anserum · LXV

57

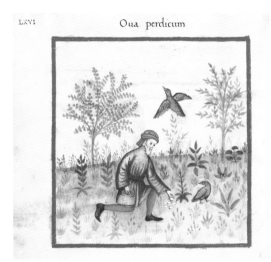

LXVI · Oua perdicum

58

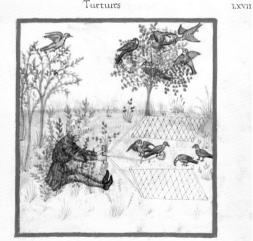

Turtures · LXVII

59

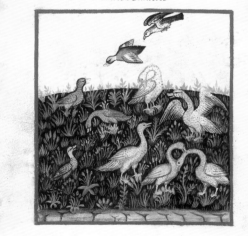

LXVIII · Anates & anseres

60

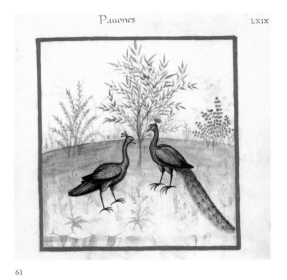

61

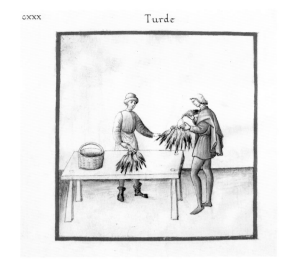

62

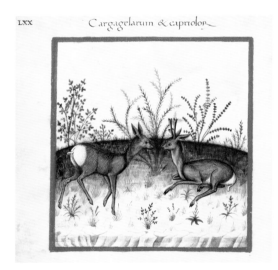

63

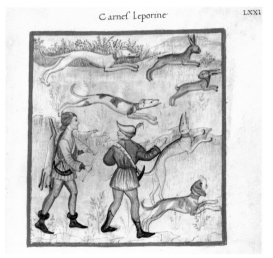

64

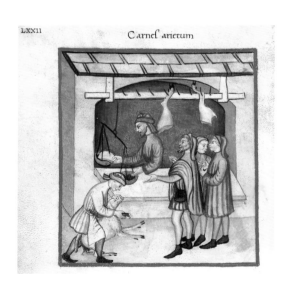

65

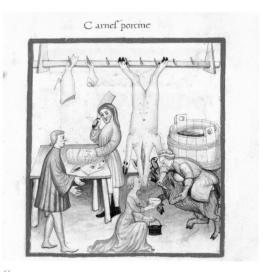

66

61 Peacocks
LXIX Pavones
A peacock and a peahen stand in a field. Peacocks can be difficult to digest, so they should be hung with weights for a period of time.

62 Thrushes
CXXX Turde
A customer selects some thrushes from a merchant's selection. The best thrushes are fat, which are good for increasing the sex drive and producing sperm.

Meat

63 Deer and goats
LXX Cargagelarum et capriolor[um]
A doe trots towards a stag, which sits in a field. *Plate 7*

64 Hare meat
LXXI Carnes leporine
Dogs chase after hares, followed closely by two hunters: this is the way to catch the best hares. Hare meat is good for the obese, and must be spiced in order to avoid insomnia.

65 Mutton
LXXII Carnes arietum
In the foreground, a butcher cuts a ram's throat. Behind him another butcher serves a group of customers, weighing a cut of meat on large scales. Two animal legs hang from a rack above the shop. The best mutton comes from animals that have been fattened for a year. Those who tend to be nauseous should not eat it.

66 Pork
LXXIX Carnes porcine
The best pork comes from young fat animals. It should be roasted and seasoned with mustard; it is very nourishing.

67 Cow and camel meat
LXXX Carnes vacine et camelor[um]
A butcher prepares an order for a customer, while one of his assistants leads in a camel. The best meat comes from young, active animals, and is good for those engaged in heavy work or who suffer from bilious complaints. It can be harmful to those who are melancholic, who should eat it with ginger and pepper. *Plate 17*

68 Goat and kid meat

LXXXV Carnes caprar[um] et p[ro]prie edor[um]

A customer examines freshly slaughtered goats hanging in a butcher shop, where a she-goat and her kid await the butcher's knife. When roasted, this meat is good for colic and is quickly digested.

69 Veal

LXXXVI Carnes vitulorum

A boy watches from a doorway as a butcher raises a mallet to stun a calf, which lies on the butcher shop floor. Nearby, another butcher prepares meat for sale. The best veal comes from newly born animals, and is good for those who do heavy work. It can be dangerous to those who suffer from disorders of the spleen, but they can neutralize its danger with exercise and baths.

70 Salted meat

LXXIII Carnes salite sicce

A customer purchases a cut of salted pork from a butcher. The legs of a recently slaughtered pig hang from a rack at the back of the shop, and another butcher carries the rest of the carcass out of the back door. The best salt meat is made from fatty animals, and it is good for those with phlegmatic temperaments and labourers. It should never be cooked with lentils, as this combination causes terrifying dreams.

71 Roasted meat

LXXIV Carnes sufrixe

A cat and her kitten look on as a woman attends to a pot of meat roasting over the kitchen fire. Because roasted meat causes thirst, it should be accompanied with wine.

Offal and meat products

72 Animal heads

LXXXIV Capita a[n]i[m]alium

A woman selects an animal's head from a display. This meat is difficult to digest and causes belching. It is good for purging the belly, and should be seasoned with cinnamon, pepper and aromatics.

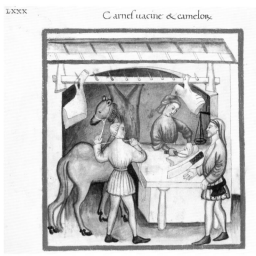

67

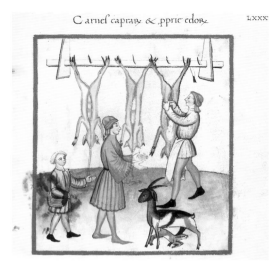

68

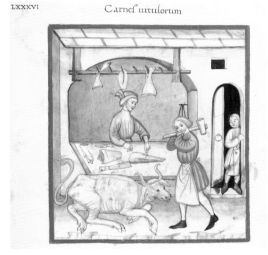

69

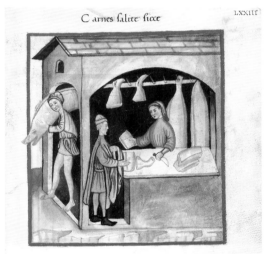

70

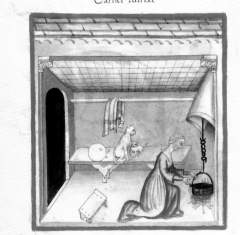

71

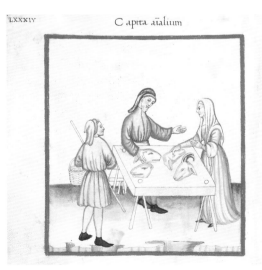

72

63

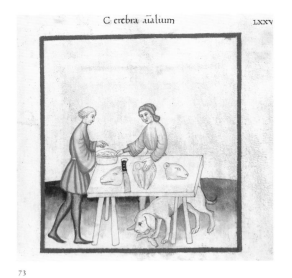

C cerebra aīalium LXXV

73

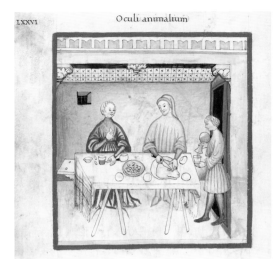

LXXVI Oculi animalium

74

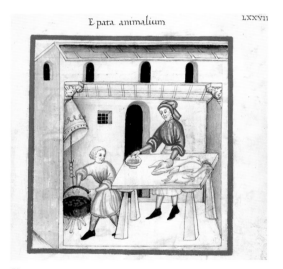

E pata animalium LXXVII

75

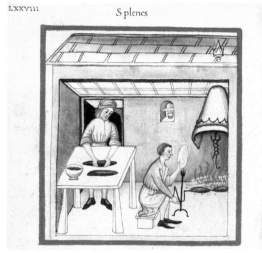

LXXVIII Splenes

76

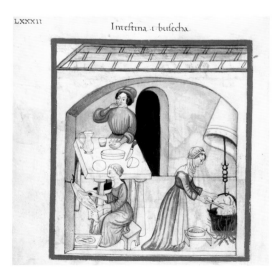

LXXXII Intestina ī busecha

77

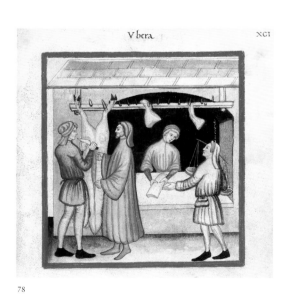

Vbera XCI

78

73 Animal brains
LXXV Cerebra a[n]i[m]alium
The best brains come from fully grown animals. They are fattening and increase the size of the eater's brain.

74 Animal eyes
LXXVI Oculi animalium
A couple enjoys a feast of animal eyes. The man pops an eye from its socket with a small knife, and the woman helps herself from a dish. A servant refills their glasses of wine. The best eyes bulge moderately. They increase the sperm, but can cause nausea and sluggish blood. They should be prepared with oregano (no. 7) and salt (no. 88).

75 Liver
LXXVII Epata animalium
The very best liver comes from geese fattened on milk and pasta, the second best comes from chicken, and the third best from pigs fattened with figs. Liver – especially from goats – is good for those who suffer from night-blindness.

76 Spleen
LXXVIII Splenes
One man rolls spleens, and another puts them on a spit. Spleens are a good food for those of fiery temperament, but they can cause a bad melancholic humour. They should come from young, fat animals, ideally pig.

77 Tripe
LXXXII Intestina i[d est] busecha
One woman sits at a low stool, and prepares the tripe by attaching it to the wall with a hook and scraping it over a dish with a knife. Another woman cooks it in a pot over a fire, while a man samples the results. The best tripe comes from ram, and helps those with digestive problems. Those with varicose veins should eat it with ginger and lots of pepper.

78 Udders
XCI Ubera
A butcher slices the udders from a cow's carcass for a waiting customer. Udders should come from a young animal. They are hard to digest, and so should be prepared with oregano (no. 7) and vinegar (no. 90).

79 Gelatine

LXXXIII Gelatina

A man scoops gelatine into a dish, while another carries a tureen of it out of the room. The best gelatine is made from fresh pigeons. It stimulates the production of bile, but can cause colic. It should be served with aromatic wine (no. 99).

80 Lard and fat

LXXXI Adeps et pinguedo

A butcher gathers the lard and fat from a pig's carcass. Fat is very nourishing, and is particularly recommended for young men and labourers.

81 Feet and shins

LXXXIX Pedes et tibie

A cook prepares for a feast of feet by scraping them with a knife, before his assistant puts them in the pot. The best are the forelegs of lambs and kids, which are good for children and the elderly. They are nutritious, and help to heal fractures. They should be boiled until the meat comes off the bone and served with vinegar (no. 90) and saffron (no. 21).

82 Hearts

XC Corda a[n]i[m]alium

Hearts should ideally come from an unweaned animal. They are nourishing, and good for the young and for labourers. They should be eaten with vinegar (no. 90), oregano (no. 7) and hyssop.

83 Testicles

XCII Testiculi

Two women stand chatting in a kitchen, while one removes testicles from rooster carcasses. The best testicles are those of fat roosters; these help to produce sperm and are very nourishing.

Fish

84 Ambergris

XCIV Ambra

Two large fish swim in a river, both apparently expelling dark round pellets. This is a probably a misunderstanding of the origin of ambergris, the precious waxy regurgitation of the sperm whale used in medieval cookery in sweet dishes, jams and custards.

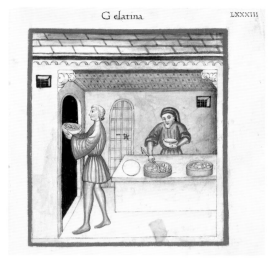

79

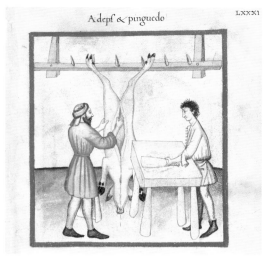

80

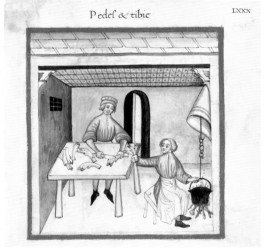

81

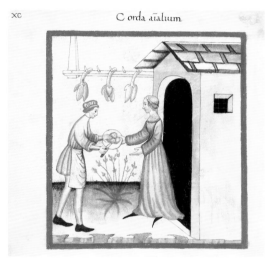

82

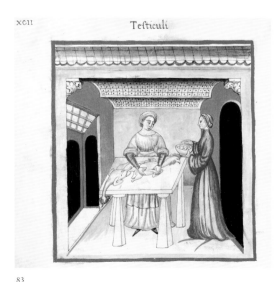

83

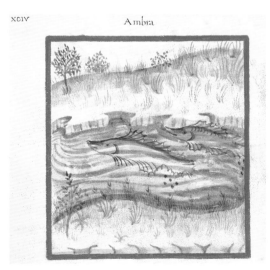

84

Gambari

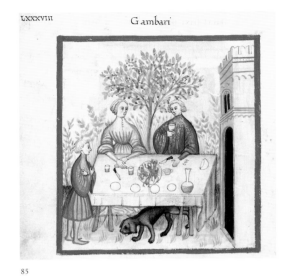

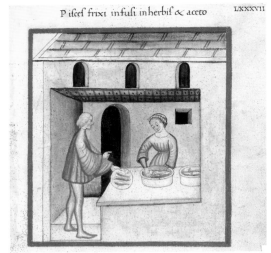

85

86

Lamprete   XCIII

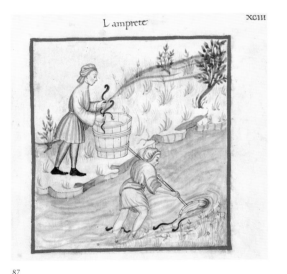

LXII   Sal

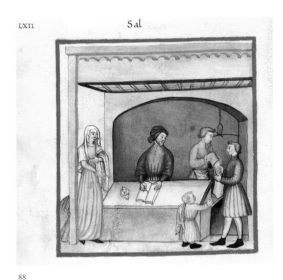

87

88

Agreste sucus   XCV

XCVI   Acetum

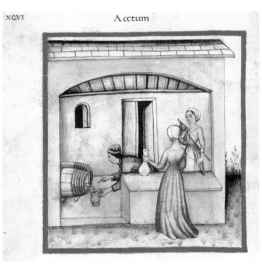

89

90

85 Crayfish
LXXXVIII Gambari
The choicest crayfish are lemon coloured, and these have aphrodisiac properties. However, they can cause drowsiness, which can be averted by sprinkling with almond oil. *Plate 12*

86 Roasted fish infused with herbs and vinegar
LXXXVII Pisces frixi infusi in herbis et aceto
A woman fills a plate with pickled fish, which should be purchased from skilled, honest fishmongers. They stimulate the appetite.

87 Lampreys
XCIII Lamprete
A man wades in shallow stream, catching lampreys in a net. On the shore, his assistant puts the wriggling fish into a bucket of water. Lampreys, which should be poached in wine with oregano (no. 7) and cloves and then fried, are fattening and nutritious.

Condiments

88 Salt
LXII Sal
A woman beckons to her child, who is busy watching a merchant fill a customer's sack with salt. The shopkeeper carefully records the transaction in a ledger. The best salt comes from the Adriatic. It aids digestion, but can cause itching and be harmful to eyesight and the brain.

89 Verjuice
XCV Agreste sucus
A woman presents a bottle of verjuice to another woman. Verjuice should be made from sour grapes, and can be used as a condiment or medication. It generates moderate humours, but can be harmful to the chest and the nerves. It should be eaten with fatty or sweet foods.

90 Vinegar
XCVI Acetum
Two women, one holding a distaff and the other an empty bottle, chat across the counter as a man fills a jug with vinegar. Vinegar should be made from good wine, and it is good for the gums and stimulates the appetite. It

can be harmful to the nerves, though, so should be taken with water and sugar.

91 Vinegar syrup
CXI Sirupus acetosus
A man purchases a small jar of vinegar syrup. The shop's shelves are full of decorated earthenware pots of various shapes and sizes. The best vinegar syrup is clear and pure, which generates cold humours. It can, however, cause coughs, dysentery and impotence. To avoid these side effects, it should be taken with sugary syrups.

92 Almond oil
CIII Oleum amigdalarum
A customer waits as a shopkeeper fills a small vial with almond oil. Almond oil is not recommended for those with weak intestines, but it is good for the stomach, chest, and coughs.

93 Olive oil
CIV Oleum olive
A man waits with a donkey burdened with large sacks as his companion delivers a sack. Olive oil softens the stomach and kills parasitic worms. It can suppress the appetite and weaken the stomach, and should always be mixed with other foods.

94 Musk
CVIII Muschus
A customer sniffs some musk from a large jar in a shop. Musk comes from gazelles found in the East. The best is dark red; this is good for the heart and brain.

95 Sugar cane
CVI Cana mellis
A man examines stalks of sugar cane, which comes from India. It is good for the blood, chest and lungs, and cures coughs and hoarseness.

96 Sugar
CVII Zucharum
A merchant weighs out sugar for a customer. The best sugar is white and clear, and it is good for the body, especially the chest, kidneys and bladder. Taking sugar with sour pomegranates will stop it from causing thirst and moving bilious humours.

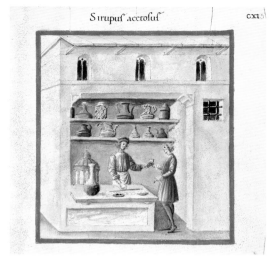

Sirupus acetosus — CXI

91

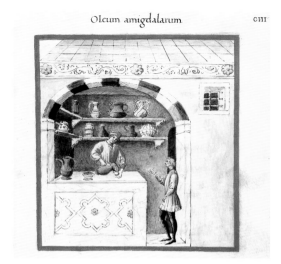

Oleum amigdalarum — CIII

92

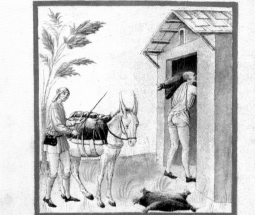

Oleum olive — CIV

93

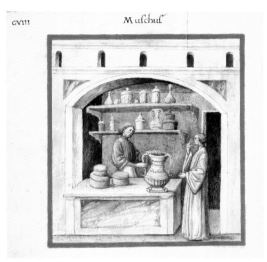

Muschus — CVIII

94

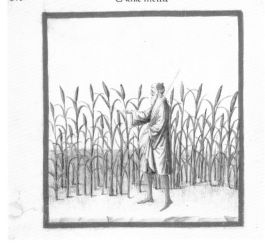

Cana mellis — CVI

95

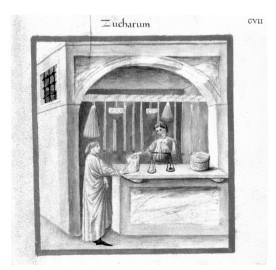

Zucharum — CVII

96

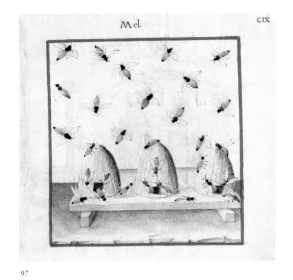

97

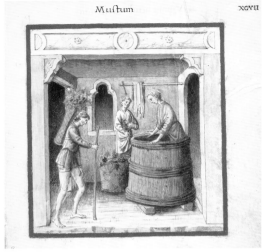

98

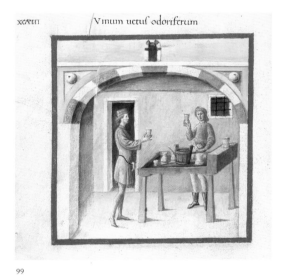

99

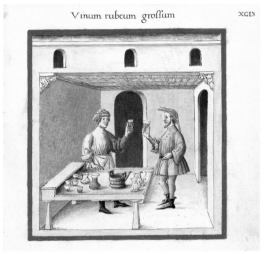

100

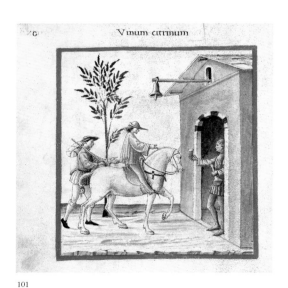

101

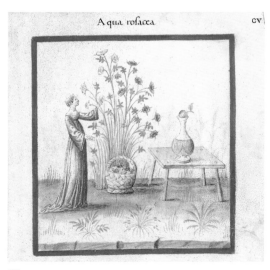

102

97 Honey
CIX Mel
Bees buzz to and from their hives. The best honey is still in the comb, which purifies and acts as a laxative. It causes thirst, so should be eaten with sour apples.

Wine

98 Must
XCVII Mustum
A man tramples grapes in a barrel, as further grapes are carried in from the vineyard. Freshly pressed grapes produce the finest must, which is fattening. Drinking it with the wine of sour pomegranates and fennel inhibits its tendency to cause flatulence.

99 Old fragrant wine
XCVIII Vinum vetus odoriferum
Two men raise their glasses, about to sample old fragrant wine. This cures eye diseases, but can be dangerous for the senses – especially for children's. Drink it alongside sour apples and lettuce hearts to avoid this.

100 Robust red wine
XCIX Vinum rubeum grossum
Judging from the profusion of empty glasses on the table, these two men are part way through a wine-tasting session. They hold up glasses of red wine to examine the colour. The most splendid red wine is the best, although it can be harmful to the liver and spleen. It should be drunk with sour pomegranates.

101 Yellow wine
C Vinum citrinum
An innkeeper offers an elegantly dressed young rider a glass of wine from a flask, presumably to refresh him after his journey. This wine reduces the danger of poisoning. Drink it with sour quince to prevent it from diminishing the appetite for sex.

Waters

102 Rose water
CV Aqua rosacea
A lady gathers rose blossoms in a basket in preparation for making rose water, which should be made from the most fragrant flowers. It is good

for the heart and prevents fainting, and should be taken with sugary syrup to avoid irritating the respiration.

103 Spring water
CI Aqua fontium
A woman returns from a spring with two buckets of water on a pole over her shoulder. Such cooling water is beneficial to the liver and digestion.

104 Salt water
CII Aqua salsa
A ship sails into a channel. Salt water is best when it is taken from a running source. Good for bathing, it frees the body but can cause itching. Put good clay in the bath to avoid this.

Seasons, winds and rooms

105 Spring
L Ver
The best part of spring falls in the middle of the season, when it is beneficial to all plants and animals. Bathing is advised, as spring can be dangerous for dirty bodies. *Plate 11*

106 Summer
XLVII Estas
The most beneficial part of summer falls at the beginning, which dissolves superfluities. To avoid digestive problems and the production of bilious humours, use moist and cooling subjects. *Plate 9*

107 Autumn
XLVIII Autumnus
Grape juice flows from a tap at the bottom of a wine barrel, in which a man is trampling grapes picked from the adjacent vine. Autumn can be dangerous to those with moderate temperaments, who should counteract its harmful effects by pouring moistening substances in the bath.

108 Winter
XLIX Hyems
A servant carries a log into a room in which a large fire is crackling away. A man with a long white beard warms himself. The best part of winter falls towards the beginning of spring. Although digestion is better in winter, it tends to generate phlegm. Counteract this by eating hot food and water, wearing warm clothing, and hot baths.

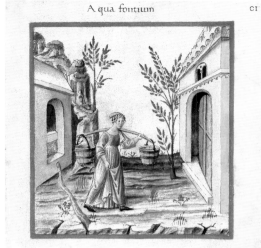

Aqua fontium — CI

103

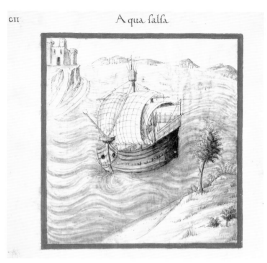

CII — Aqua salsa

104

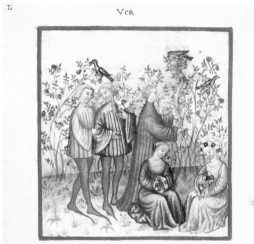

L — Ver

105

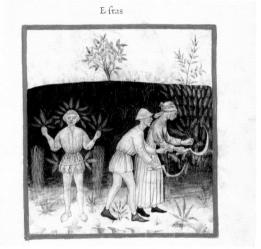

Estas

106

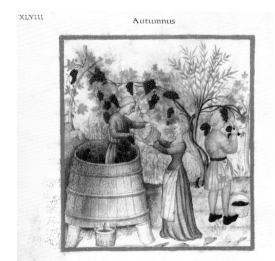

XLVIII — Autumnus

107

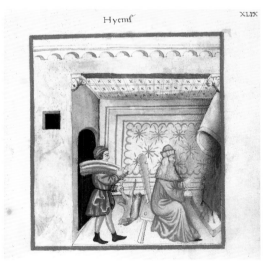

Hyems — XLIX

108

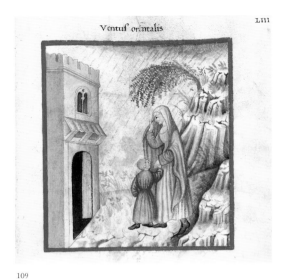

109

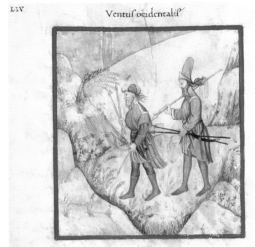

110

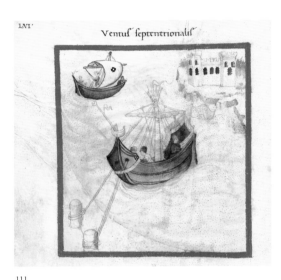

111

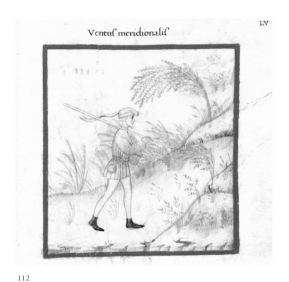

112

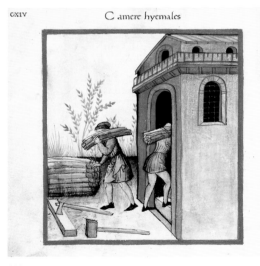

113

114

109 The east wind

LIII Ventus orientalis

A woman hurries home, shielding herself and her little boy from the rain with her cloak. The easterly wind brings rain, which raises the spirits but can cause diseases of the eyes and heart.

110 The west wind

LIV Ventus ocidentalis

Two hunters trek through a hilly landscape, impervious to the gusting west wind. This wind aids digestion, but causes shivering and colds.

111 The north wind

LVI. Ventus septentrionalis

A ship strains at its moorings as another takes advantage of the wind and sails away. The north wind sharpens the senses, but can cause coughing. Hot baths and heavy clothing are recommended.

112 The south wind

LV Ventus meridionalis

A traveller walks into the wind. The south wind is good for the chest, but dulls the senses. Baths are recommended.

113 Summer rooms

CXIII Camere estivales

A young couple converse among the columns of an open loggia. Such summer rooms are able to bring one's constitutional elements and the digestive system to the same temperature.

114 Winter rooms

CXIV Camere hyemales

Two men prepare a supply of fuel for the winter fire. Winter rooms should be heated to the temperature of the air at the end of spring in order to awaken faculties. These rooms should face north, otherwise they cause thirst and poor digestion.

Emotions, sleep, activities and clothing

115 Anger

CXVI Ira

A man raises an admonishing finger to an angry woman, who bites a cloth to stifle her fury. The most advantageous kind of anger restores evanescent colour, and can be good for paralysis and mouth pains. However, it can cause trembling, fever and anxiety, and it is dangerous for those prone to make illicit decisions. Philosophy offers the best way to neutralize these dangers.

116 Modesty
CXV Verecondia
Two elegantly dressed young men stand together, as an older man addresses a blushing girl. Modesty is best suited to those with temperate constitutions and to teenagers. Discretion neutralizes its harmful effects.

* 117 A betrothed woman
CXXVI Sponsa
A well-dressed young couple stand in a flower garden and touch one another tenderly.

118 Drunkenness
CXVII Ebrietas
Three men drink wine and play dice. Drunkenness is caused by drinking too much wine. It is good for severe pain, and prevents the deterioration of the humours. It can result in heaviness of the brain. Vomiting and nourishing food can counteract its negative effects.

119 Vomiting
CXVIII Vomitus
A woman watches as a lady holds the head of a man while he vomits. Vomiting can be beneficial for an overstuffed stomach, but it can be bad for the brain and for those with narrow chests. The best way to neutralize these dangers is to blindfold the sufferer and to use an appropriate apparatus.

120 Conversation
CXIX Confabulator
A group of people converse by a fire; a sleepy boy rests his head on his hand. Conversation should be pleasurable, which helps with the digestion and causes sleep. It can be harmful to listen to many people rather than just one, so silence should be imposed on others. It is good for everyone except small children. Conversation can be tedious: the remedy for this is sleep.

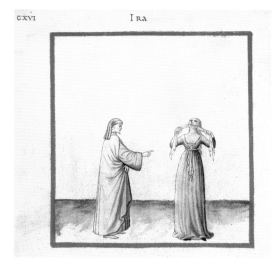

115

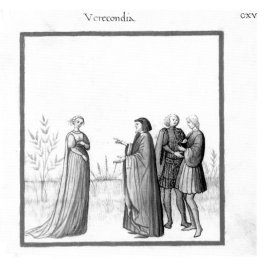

116

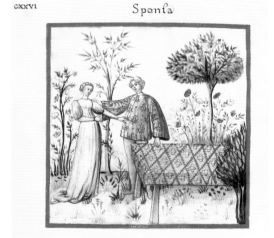

117

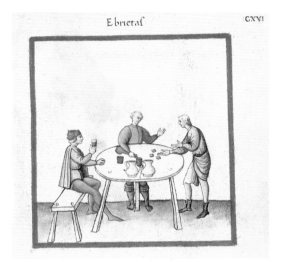

118

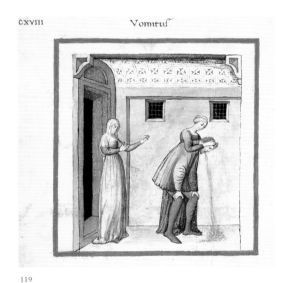

119

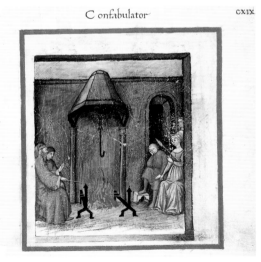

120

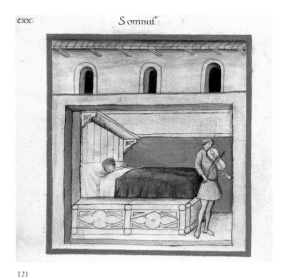

121

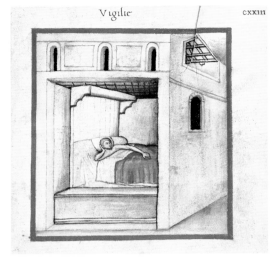

122

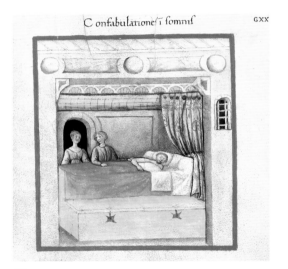

123

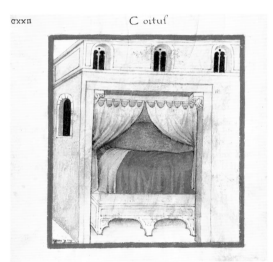

124

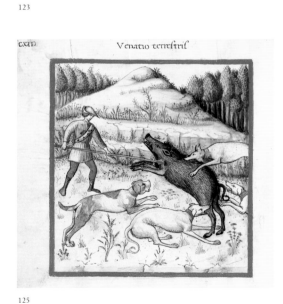

125

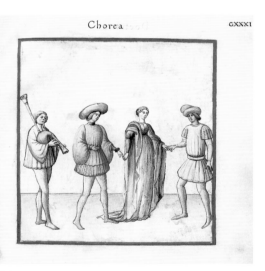

126

121 Sleep
CXX Somnus

A musician plays soothing music to a man asleep in bed. One should sleep for eight hours at night. Too much sleep dries out the body, and can cause weakness because it brings an empty stomach. Sleep during the day should be avoided. *Plate 15*

122 Insomnia
CXXIII Vigilie

A man lies in bed with his head propped up on his elbow, unable to sleep. Insomnia can be useful for thinking about things of vital importance, but too much wakefulness can tire the senses, cause circles under the eyes, and arouse anger. The remedy for this is sleep.

123 Sleep-talking
CXXI Confabulatione i[n] somnis

Two women listen to a man talking in his sleep. Sleep-talking can be dangerous because one might make rude remarks; it is best to say things that are pleasant to hear. *Plate 18*

124 Sex
CXXII Coitus

A couple has sex, their privacy ensured by thick blankets. Sex is useful for preserving the species, and it is best when the sperm has been completely emitted. Sperm-producing foods prevent it from being harmful to those with cold and dry breathing.

125 Hunting
CXII Venatio terrestris

A hunter spears a boar in the breast while his dogs attack. The ideal form of hunting is the easiest kind, which thins the humours. It can dry out the body, so oiling the body while bathing is recommended.

126 Dancing
CXXXI Chorea

A bagpiper plays to two men and a lady as they dance. It is beneficial to move the body in time to music, but it is also good joyfully to observe dancing and singing. The only danger is if the tempo is lost.

127 Singing

CXXV Cantus

Two priests and two novices prepare to sing from a large choir-book resting on a lectern. The best singing engages the hearts of the listeners, and can prevent illness.

128 Singing and playing musical instruments

CXXIV Organizare cantu et pulsare

Musicians playing a viol and a portable organ accompany a singer. Sweet singing is enjoyable, but if it is too subdued or out of tune, it is irritating.

* 129 Instruction

CXXXII Doctrina

A gentleman points out a tree to his young companion, while they stroll arm in arm.

130 Cloth

CXXVII Panni

A tailor unfolds a bolt of fabric for a client. New clothes hang over a rail above the workbench, and two young assistants sit with their work across their knees. This same blue fabric patterned with red turns up several times in these illustrations, as curtains (no. 123) and as the tunics worn by a bridegroom (no. 117) and picnicker (no. 85).

131 Tailor

CXXVIII Sartor

A tailor inspects the hemline of a customer's wool tunic. The finest kind of wool comes from Flanders and is lightweight. It can irritate the skin, so should be lined with linen.

132 Linen

CXXIX Lintea

A group of women make clothes from linen. One cuts the cloth with scissors, and others sit on low stools with their work across their knees. The best variety of linen is that which is splendid and beautiful. It regulates the heat of the body, but if it presses down on the skin it can prevent perspiration. To avoid this it should be blended with silk. It is particularly recommended for those with hot temperaments, the summer months, and for those who live in the south.

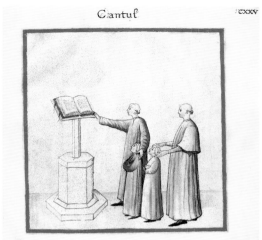

Cantus · CXXV

127

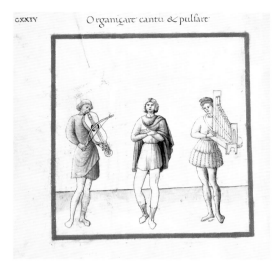

CXXIV · Organizare cantu & pulsare

128

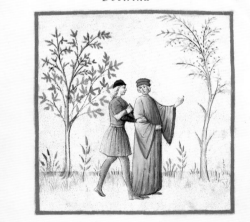

CXXXII · Doctrina

129

Panni · CXXVII

130

Sartor · CXXVIII

131

Lintea · CXXIX

132

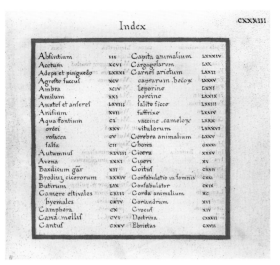

133

134

133 Index
CXXXIII
When the Liechtenstein-Rouen *Tacuinum* was divided into two, the Liechtenstein portion was given page numbers in Roman numerals and furnished with this index. Both the page numbers and the index are written in a script that imitates the humanist hand of the scribe who copied the manuscript in the 1450s. *Absintium-Ebrietas* (see also no. 134).

134 Index
CXXXIV and CXXXV
The 19th-century index, *Epata animalium-Zucharum.*

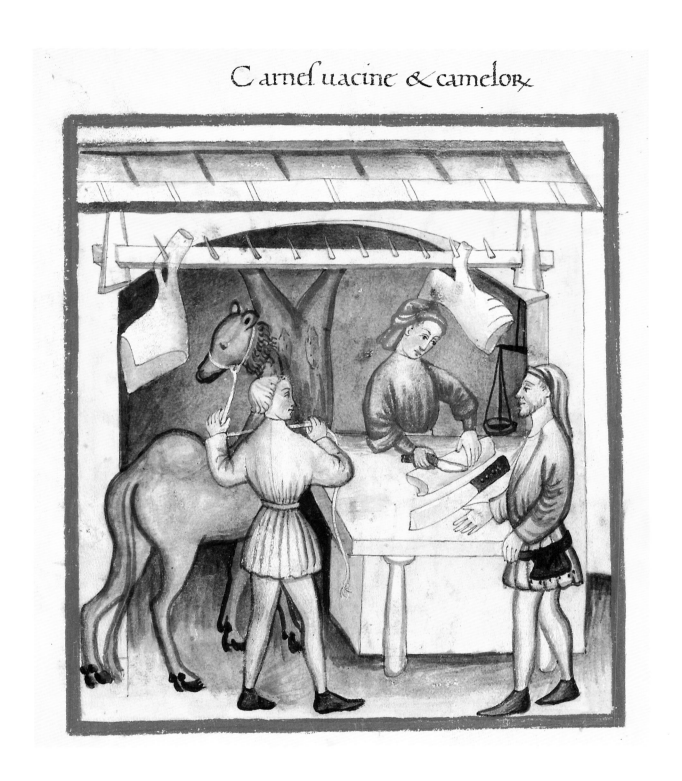

Carnes uacine & camelor

PLATE 17 **Cows and camel meat**

Reflecting the Arabic source of the *Tacuinum*, this miniature shows a camel wearing a bridle being led into a butcher shop. Camel meat – undoubtedly an exotic delicacy in fifteenth-century Padua – has the same medicinal effects as that of cow. Neither cow nor camel are recommended for the melancholy, unless they are spiced with ginger and pepper. *No. 67*

Select Bibliography

The following is intended to help the general reader navigate the substantial literature that is relevant to the Liechtenstein *Tacuinum Sanitatis*. I have tried to focus on recent publications that contain further bibliography, but inevitably some of the material cited here may be difficult to locate without recourse to a specialist library. Details of the sources of information used in the essay are provided in the endnotes (pp. 35–36).

The fundamental study of the *Tacuinum Sanitatis* remains Luisa Cogliati Arano, *The Medieval Health Handbook: Tacuinum Sanitatis* (New York, 1976), which includes a detailed bibliography and a helpful historiographic survey. The catalogue section of the Italian edition includes more pictorial and textual information than its English counterpart (Luisa Cogliati Arano, *Tacuinum Sanitatis*, Milan, 1973). While the Rouen manuscript is included in Cogliati Arano's study, the Liechtenstein *Tacuinum* is not. Other groundbreaking discussions of the *Tacuina* include Otto Pächt, 'Early Italian Nature Studies,' *Journal of the Courtauld and Warburg Institutes* 13 (1950), pp. 13–47, and Brucia Whittoft, 'The *Tacuinum Sanitatis*: A Lombard Panorama,' *Gesta* 17 (1978), pp. 49–60. For an up-to-date view of the Paris *Tacuinum* see Florence Moly Mariotti, 'Le Ricette del Benessere: Il *Tacuinum Sanitatis* della Bibliothèque Nationale di Parigi', *Alumina* 8 (2005), pp. 4–12.

All of the copies of illustrated *Tacuinum Sanitatis* manuscripts (except the Liechtenstein-Rouen copy) have been published in facsimile, sometimes more than once: details of these publications can be found on p. 35 in notes 13–16. Many of the images in the Vienna *Tacuinum* are included in *The Four Seasons of the House of Cerruti*, trans. Judith Spencer (New York, 1984). The Vienna *Tacuinum* is also featured in Werner Telesko, *The Wisdom of Nature: The Healing Powers and Symbolism of Plants and Animals in the Middle Ages* (Munich, 2001).

The first publication that included images of the Liechtenstein *Tacuinum* is Victor Gay, *Glossaire Archéologique du Moyen Age et de la Renaissance* (Paris, 1887), pp. 154, 169, 200, and 483. It has been published most frequently in sale catalogues. The New York book dealer H.P. Kraus owned the Liechtenstein *Tacuinum* twice, and published it in two of his catalogues, *Catalogue 59* (1951), no. 33, and *Catalogue 165*, entitled *Cimelia: A Catalogue of Important Illuminated and Textual Manuscripts Published in Commemoration of the Sale of the Ludwig Collection* (New York, 1983), no. 7. It was also included in a book featuring the top one hundred manuscripts that passed through his hands: H.P. Kraus, *In Retrospect: A Catalogue of 100 Outstanding Manuscripts Sold in the Last Four Decades by H.P. Kraus* (New York, 1978), no. 50. For the story of how Kraus acquired the *Tacuinum*, see H.P. Kraus, *A Rare Book Saga: The Autobiography of H.P. Kraus* (London, 1979), p. 153. The Liechtenstein *Tacuinum* has passed through Sotheby's sale rooms twice –

Sotheby's, New York, 30 October 1981, lot 48, and Sotheby's, London, 17 December 1991, lot 50. Both catalogue descriptions include much useful information.

Recent studies drawing specifically on the Liechtenstein *Tacuinum* include Florence Moly Mariotti, 'Contribution à la connaissance des *Tacuina sanitatis* lombards,' *Arte Lombarda* (1993), pp. 32–39, and Agnes Acolos Bertiz's PhD dissertation, 'Picturing Health: The Garden and Courtiers at Play in the Late Fourteenth-Century Illuminated *Tacuinum Sanitatis*', PhD thesis, University of Southern Carolina (2003), which provides much useful information. Bertiz revised the concordance published by Cogliati Arano and added the Liechtenstein *Tacuinum* to it. The Liechtenstein *Tacuinum* was exhibited in 1995 in *Princely Taste: Treasures from Great Private Collections* (The Israel Museum, Jerusalem, 1995), p. 83.

For an edition of Arabic *Taqwim* with a French translation, see Hosam Elkhadem, *Le Taqwīm al-Ṣiḥḥa (Tacuini Sanitatis) d'Ibn Buṭlān: un traité médical du XIᵉ siècle. Histoire du texte, édition critique, traduction, commentaire* (Louvain, 1990). Lawrence I. Conrad, 'Scholarship and social context: a medical case from the eleventh-century Near East', in *Knowledge and the Scholarly Medical Traditions*, ed. Don Bates (Cambridge, 1995), pp. 84–100, is a fascinating account of an episode in the career of the *Taqwīm*'s author, Ibn Buṭlān.

For an erudite and highly readable introduction to the history of medicine, see Roy Porter, *The Greatest Benefit to Mankind: A Medical History of Humanity from Antiquity to the Present* (London, 1997). *The Western Medical Tradition 800 BC to AD 1800*, ed. Lawrence I. Conrad, Michael Neve, Vivian Nutton, Roy Porter and Andrew Wear (Cambridge, 1995) includes chapters focusing on Late Antiquity, the Arab-Islamic tradition and the Middle Ages and Renaissance. For helpful introductions to Renaissance medicine, see Nancy G. Siraisi, *Medieval and Early Renaissance Medicine: An Introduction to Knowledge and Practise* (Chicago, 1990) and Katharine Park, *Doctors and Medicine in Early Renaissance Florence* (Princeton, NJ, 1985). A useful account of hygienic literature that touches on the *Tacuinum Sanitatis* is Pedro Gil Sotres, 'The Regimens of Health', in *Western Medical Thought from Antiquity to the Middle Ages*, ed. Mirko D. Grmek (Harvard, 1998), pp. 291–318. For a history of diet and cookery that draws on the *Tacuinum*, see Terence Scully, *The Art of Cookery in the Middle Ages* (Woodbridge, Suffolk, 1995).

Peter Murray Jones, *Medieval Medicine in Illuminated Manuscripts* (London, 1998) provides an excellent and well-illustrated overview of the manuscript tradition, while Loren MacKinney, *Medical Illustrations in Medieval Manuscripts* (London, 1965) remains extremely useful. The best introduction to Herbals is Minta Collins, *Medieval Herbals: The Illustrative Traditions* (London and Toronto, 2000).

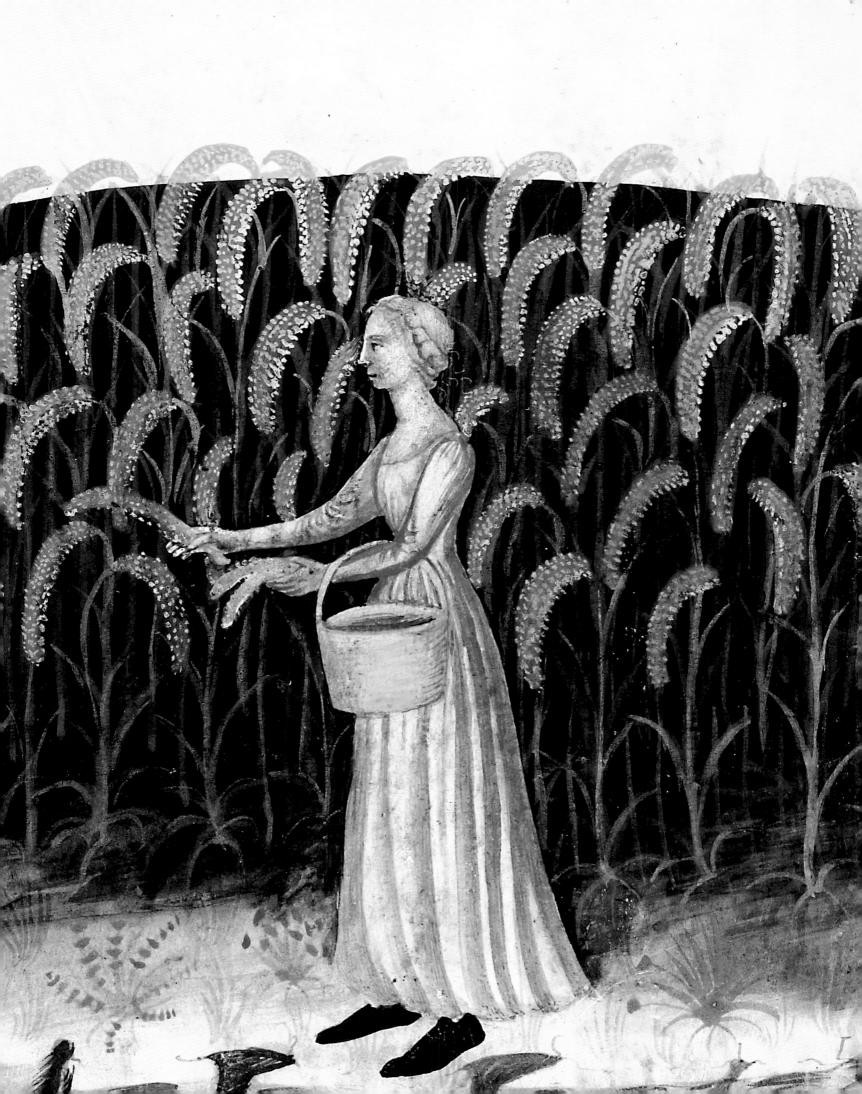

Subject Index of the Liechtenstein *Tacuinum*

About the Author

Alixe Bovey's publications include *Monsters and Grotesques in Medieval Manuscripts* (British Library/ University of Toronto, 2002) and *The Chaworth Roll: A Fourteenth-Century Genealogy of the Kings of England* (Sam Fogg, 2005). She is currently completing *The Smithfield Decretals: Tales from the Margins of a Fourteenth-Century Law Book* (British Library/ University of Toronto, forthcoming). She received her doctorate from the Courtauld Institute of Art, has worked as a curator in the British Library's Department of Manuscripts, and lives in London with her husband and daughter.

Acknowledgements

I owe thanks to many friends and colleagues who have generously contributed to this project. I owe particular thanks to Laura Nuvoloni for providing much advice, sharing her extensive knowledge of Paduan scribes and illuminators, and making many insightful comments on a draft of the text. Tony Edwards was generous with his time and advice, and Crofton Black and Will Kwiatkowski provided much useful advice on aspects of the Arabic tradition. Additionally, Tony and Crofton made many constructive comments on the text. Claire Breay, Caroline Campbell, Hugo Chapman, Jo Kirby and Helen Loveday kindly shared their time and expertise. Christelle Quillet, Conservateur-adjoint chargé du patrimoine, of the Rouen Bibliothèque municipale, kindly answered many questions regarding the Rouen *Tacuinum*. The professionalism and good humour of Roger Davies, Sam Fogg, Paul Holberton, Annick Lapôtre, Charlotte Lochhead and Liza Lowell made this project not only feasible but enjoyable, and the kindness and support of my husband Jeremy Phillips enabled me to work to a tight deadline. I have relied, as ever, on the remarkable collections of the Warburg Institute, the Courtauld Institute and the British Library.

Photo Credits

Albi, Bibliothèque municipale (fig. 23). Liechtenstein *Tacuinum*: Matt Pia. London, British Library (figs. 2, 8, 24). Milan, Biblioteca Ambrosiana (fig. 4). Paris, Bibliothèque Nationale de France (fig. 5). Rome, Biblioteca Casanatense (fig. 7). Rouen, Bibliothèque municipale (figs. 1, 7, 10, 11, 21, 22). Vienna, Österreichische Nationalbibliothek (figs. 6, 18, 19).

Colophon

Front cover: *Turnips*, no. 27 (detail)
Back cover: *Spring*, no. 105 (detail)
Page 1: *Hunting*, no. 125 (detail)
Page 2: *Hens' eggs*, no. 56 (detail)
Page 4: *Autumn*, no. 107 (detail)
Page 37: *Flax*, no. 49 (detail)
Page 47: *Liquorice*, no. 15 (detail)
Page 77: *Panic grass*, no. 41 (detail)

Photography: Matt Pia

Design: Roger Davies
daviesdesign@onetel.com

Produced by
Paul Holberton publishing
37 Snowsfields, London SE1 3SU
www.paul-holberton.net

Printed in Italy by Graphic Studio, Bussolengo, Verona

ISBN 0-9549014-3-6
Copyright © 2005 Sam Fogg

Distributed in Europe by Paul Holberton publishing, and in the United States and Canada for Paul Holberton publishing by University of Washington Press

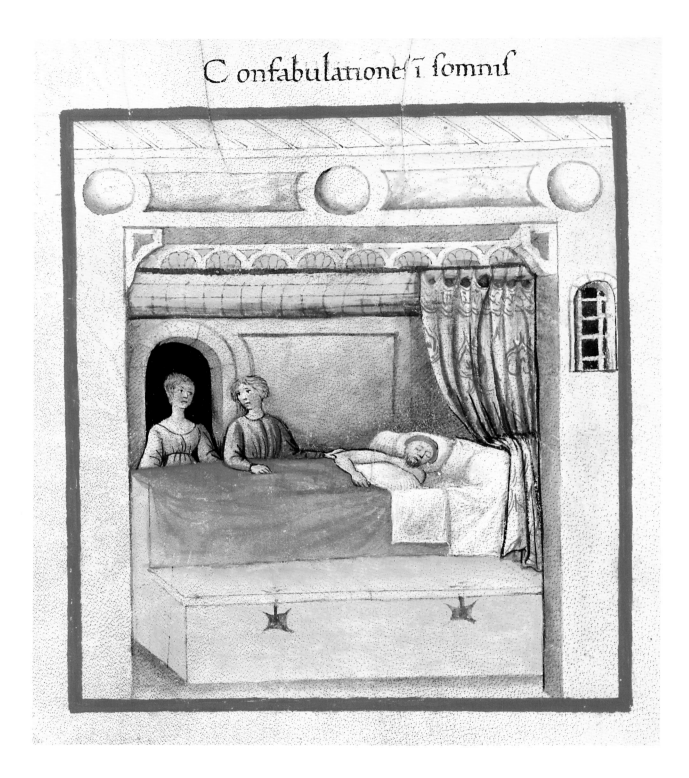

Confabulatione īn somnis

PLATE 18 **Sleep talking**

The problem with sleep talking, according to the *Tacuinum*, is that others might overhear unpleasant things uttered by the sleeper. This image shows two women standing by a bed, listening attentively in case the sleeping man mutters anything of interest. *No. 123*